THE M. & E. HANDBOOK SERIES

BASIC ECONOMICS

G. L. THIRKETTLE
B. Com. (Lond.), F.I.S.
Formerly Senior Lecturer, Polytechnic of North London

THIRD EDITION

MACDONALD & EVANS LTD
8 John Street, London WC1N 2HY

First published January 1965
Reprinted September 1965
Reprinted April 1966
Reprinted June 1967
Reprinted May 1968
Reprinted January 1969
Reprinted February 1970
Second Edition June 1971
Reprinted October 1972
Reprinted March 1974
Third Edition October 1975

ISBN 0 7121 0249 3

©

MACDONALD AND EVANS LIMITED
1975

*Printed in Great Britain by Richard Clay (The Chaucer Press), Ltd.,
Bungay, Suffolk*

PREFACE TO THE THIRD EDITION

THESE study notes are intended for use by students preparing for *intermediate professional* examinations in banking, accounting, company secretaryship, transport, building society administration, etc., and for students preparing for the *G.C.E.* *"A" level* examination in Economics. They also cover *certain final professional* examinations.

The study notes are comprehensive and in conjunction with the Progress Tests provide a self-contained course. The book should also prove useful for revision, which must, of course, be a continuous process.

In this new edition the text has been enlarged by the addition of a number of topics that are now of examination importance. The statistics have been updated, in particular, those relating to the National Income, and the Balance of Payments, where considerable changes in presentation have been introduced. There are also many minor revisions.

Method of study. Study each chapter in turn and in the same order as in the book; do not pass on to a new chapter until you have satisfactorily dealt with the current one, that is, until you can answer all the questions in the Progress Test at the end of the chapter without reference to the book.

First read through the chapter to get a general idea of what it is about. Then read it in detail, section by section, and this time learn the subject matter. Certain paragraphs may require reading a number of times before they can be mastered. Finally, test yourself by means of the Progress Tests. Jot down answers without referring to the study notes. Check yourself by means of the reference given after each question.

Test papers and examination technique. At the end of the book is an Appendix on technique in Economics examinations, followed by several three-hour test papers. Do not attempt any of these until you have read the hints on examination technique and do not do any test until you have achieved complete confidence in answering the Progress Tests at the end of each chapter.

Progress Tests. These enable the student to ensure that he has done all the necessary study to enter the examination room with confidence. Examiners frequently report that too many candidates attempt the examination with insufficient preparation.

From time to time a warning, denoted by a star (∗), has been given on topics where experience has shown students are prone to error. Extra care is needed in these cases.

Acknowledgments. I thank The Institute of Chartered Secretaries and Administrators, the Institute of Bankers and the Senate of the University of London for permission to reproduce past examination questions.

May 1975   G. L. THIRKETTLE

NOTICE TO LECTURERS

More and more lecturers are now using **HANDBOOKS** as working texts to save time otherwise wasted by students in protracted note-taking. The purpose of the series is to meet practical teaching requirements as far as possible, and lecturers are cordially invited to forward comments or criticisms to the Publishers for consideration.

P. W. D. REDMOND
General Editor

CONTENTS

LIST OF FIGURES

LIST OF TABLES

CHAPTER I

THE NATURE OF ECONOMICS

1. The meaning of economics. We are all practising economists, having to make the best of our limited incomes. They are limited (however large) in the sense that they are insufficient to buy all we want and a choice has to be made. The acquisition of one commodity or service means that some other commodity or service is not bought. Limited incomes compete for alternatives. We so arrange to spend our income that the amount of satisfaction we get from it is as great as possible. We do not always succeed in doing this, but it is our aim. This act of *economising*, getting the most out of any given income, shows man in his rôle as a *consumer*. The principles dealing with the way in which income is spent and saved are part of the subject matter of economics.

An income is obtained either by (*a*) working, that is, providing *labour*, or (*b*) owning property (such as a combine harvester or a blast furnace), that is, providing *capital*, or (*c*) both.

Capital and labour are known as *factors of production*. They are used to produce the goods and services man requires (*e.g.* wheat, steel). In providing these resources of capital and labour man plays the rôle of a *producer*. Resources are *scarce*, in the sense that not all that is wanted can be produced. The production of one commodity or service means the forgoing of some alternative. If office blocks are built, then houses which could have been built with the same resources are not built. A choice has to be made—again, *scarcity and choice*. Furthermore, there is the problem of getting the maximum satisfaction out of given resources. The principles governing the allocation of scarce resources among competing uses is also part of the subject matter of economics.

> * Man is both consumer and producer. As a producer he earns an income; as a consumer he spends it. As a producer he provides resources; as a consumer he uses up goods and services.

Price plays a large part in determining how a person spends his income; it also affects what is produced. Price is in fact the

1

regulator (not a perfect one) which causes those things to be produced which people want produced. The working of this *price mechanism* is a central part of the study of economics: *see* Chapters VII, VIII, IX, *and* X.

Micro-economics deals with the question of how the prices of individual goods or resources are determined: *see* Chapters VII–XIV.

Macro-economics deals with "totals"; for example, the general level of all prices (Chapter XV). It is mainly concerned, however, with the determination of total incomes and employment (Chapter XXII).

2. The pattern of economic activity. Refer to Fig. 1, "The economic process." The term PERSONS represents all those people who pursue economic activities, providing productive resources (factors of production) in return for *money incomes* (wages, salaries, profits, dividends, rent). They spend their money incomes on goods and services, thus changing their money incomes into *real incomes*. The goods and services people buy to enjoy their use (food, clothes, cameras, tickets for entertainment, etc.) are called *consumption goods*.

The people are of all kinds—dustmen, actors, sailors, clerks, and directors making policy decisions. These people provide labour. Then there are the landlords and the shareholders who own the property of various companies; they get their income from the use made of their *capital*.

* *Capital* consists of goods, materials, machines, etc., not wanted as consumption goods but used to produce consumption goods and services. The actual property is called *real capital* to distinguish it from *money capital*—the latter being a sum of money available to purchase or hire real capital.

The term FIRMS in Fig. 1 represents production units. A *production unit* is the establishment (shop, factory, plant, field) where production takes place, where the factors of production (work of various kinds, including managerial administration, raw materials, capital such as factory buildings and machines) are combined and changed into commodities and services. This act of changing *inputs* of factors of production into *outputs* of goods and services is *production*.

The *economic process* consists of persons providing factors of production to firms in return for money incomes. The firms receive these factors of production, for which they pay (the

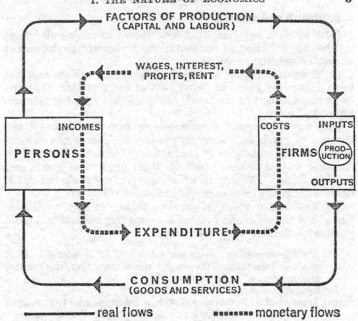

FIG. 1.—*The economic process.*

cost is known as *factor cost* and is the same as incomes of persons); the firms produce goods and services whose total cost gives the money value of the total product produced; Persons spend their incomes on the goods and services produced by the firms.

$$\text{TOTAL INCOMES OF PERSONS} = \text{TOTAL PRODUCT AT FACTOR COST} = \text{TOTAL EXPENDITURE}$$

There are two flows in opposite directions:

1. A *monetary flow*: money flowing from firms to persons (firms purchasing factors of production) and then from persons back to firms (persons purchasing goods and services from firms).
2. A *"real" flow*: factors of production flowing from persons to firms and then, after being changed into goods and services, flowing back to persons.

3. Wealth and welfare.

(a) *Welfare* is anything that contributes to one's well-being, *e.g.* health, a feeling of contentment, a pleasant environment as well as wealth: *see below*.

(b) *Economic welfare* is a part of this total welfare and has been defined by Pigou as "that part of social welfare that can be brought directly or indirectly into relation with the measuring rod of money."

One way of increasing economic welfare is to increase the amount of goods and services produced. This is the subject matter of the *economics of production* (Chapters III *and* IV). Another way is to share out the total product of goods and services fairly. The way in which the product is shared out is dealt with in the *economics of distribution* (Chapters XI–XIV).

(c) *Wealth* is a stock of goods existing at any particular time. For an economist to consider anything as wealth it must possess *all* the following attributes:

  (i) *Utility:* anything possesses utility if it is wanted, if it gives satisfaction. The greater the satisfaction, the greater the amount of utility it has.
  (ii) *Supply limited.*
  (iii) *Money value:* however valuable a thing may be (*e.g.* rain or air, without which life is not possible), if it does not possess a money value the economist does not include it as wealth.
  (iv) *Ownership transferable.*

  ∗ A commodity or service only has value if it is exchangeable for other commodities or services or for money.

  ∗ Money is *not* wealth, but a claim to wealth (for the meaning and functions of money, *see* Chapter XV, 1 *and* 2).

(d) *Individual wealth* includes both personal goods (clothes, furniture, houses, etc.) and any share in the property of a business. It includes money and debts receivable, less debts owed.

(e) *National wealth* includes the whole stock of goods within a country, those owned by individuals and those owned by the community. It includes debts due from other countries and any foreign currencies owned, less debts owed to other countries and sterling (English money) owned by them. It does *not* include sterling nor debts owned internally, since wealth cannot be increased by printing more notes or increasing loans to one another.

4. Economic problems. These arise because of scarcity; the income of an individual and the resources of a community are both limited, and all wants cannot be satisfied. Goods are scarce relative to wants: a choice must be made.

(a) *Problems of an individual.* These include:

(i) division of time between work and leisure,
(ii) choice of job,
(iii) how much of one's income to spend and how much to save,
(iv) allocation of expenditure among the various goods and services,
(v) in what form to keep wealth (goods? money? shares? etc.).

(b) *Problems of the community.* These include:

(i) what goods and services to produce and in what quantities,
(ii) how to allocate the available resources among the production units,
(iii) how the product is to be allocated among the members of the community,
(iv) what provision to make for the growth of the community; what proportion of the goods made shall be capital goods and what proportion consumption goods.

* An economic problem must be distinguished from a technical one. An *economic problem* deals with the allocation of scarce resources among *competing ends* (*e.g.* factories *or* a Channel tunnel). A technical problem deals with how best to attain a given end (*e.g.* having chosen to build a Channel tunnel, should it be on the sea bed or under the sea bed?).

5. Economic systems. The particular economic system of any country will depend upon who owns its wealth, the individual or the State. There are three basic types of system:

(a) *Free enterprise* (also known as *laisser-faire*). All wealth is owned by individuals and the economic problems of the community are solved through the price mechanism system (changes in consumers' wants lead to changes in prices: Chapter X. Changes in prices lead to changes in supply: Chapter IX. Changes in wants therefore lead to changes in supply.) It is the "consumers' sovereignty" system.

(b) *Planned economy.* The problems of production (what and how much), distribution (to whom and how much), and growth are solved by a central planning authority—the State.

(c) *Mixed economy.* In a free enterprise system the economic decisions are made by individuals; in a planned
economy by the State; in a mixed economy some decisions are made by the State (the public sector) and some
by individuals (the private sector).

The U.S.S.R. is an example of a planned economy. The
U.K. is an example of a mixed economy. There is no example
of a completely free enterprise system. There is a tendency
in all mixed economies for the public sector to grow at the
expense of the private sector.

6. Economic policy. The aims of economic policy for all
modern governments are:

(a) to *improve the standard of living* by increasing the national
product,
(b) to *ensure full employment* so that men and resources are
not idle and production lower than it need be,
(c) to *lessen economic inequality,*
(d) to *provide social security,*
(e) to *ensure equilibrium of the balance of payments* (*i.e.* that
there are sufficient exports to pay for imports: Chapter
XIX),
(f) to *provide for the future of the economy and its growth.*

7. Economics as a science. Lord Robbins has defined
economics as "*the science which studies human behaviour as a
relationship between ends and scarce means which have alternative
uses.*"

It is a *social science* dealing with economic choices. A
social science is one dealing with man's actions as a social
being (other social sciences include ethics, psychology, etc.).

It is a *positive science*; that is, it attempts to explain economic life as it is, not as it ought to be.

Economics is a science because it formulates generalisations
concerning the relationship between observed facts. Such a
generalisation is a scientific law. As an example of such a law
in economics, the general law of demand may be cited: "the
lower the price, the greater the amount bought." It is of the
form: "if A, then B."

Most economic laws are statements of tendencies, and
assume that matters not being considered and which would
influence the result are not present (the assumption of *ceteris*

paribus). In the case just mentioned it is assumed, among other assumptions, that incomes have not fallen.

There are two *methods of reasoning* employed in science. They are:

(a) *Induction.* Facts are collected, classified, and a generalisation made from them. It has been observed that in a large number of cases the greater a person's income the smaller the proportion of that income spent on food. Engel's law states that the proportion of expenditure spent on food falls as total expenditure increases. This is an example of inductive reasoning.

(b) *Deduction.* In the deductive method the starting point is to take certain accepted hypotheses and to reason from these assumptions to other propositions. From the generally accepted assumption that less and less satisfaction is obtained from successive increments of any commodity it can be reasoned that if the price of the commodity falls more of it will be bought (Chapter VII, 4). This is an example of deductive reasoning.

Economists often disagree about the effects of certain policies (*e.g.* whether it was to the economic advantage of the U.K. to enter the Common Market) because they start off from different assumptions.

    * Frequent fallacies met in economics:

(i) "*Post hoc, ergo propter hoc,*" *i.e.* assuming that if A occurs after B, it is caused by B. For instance if prices rise after nationalisation, to assume that they rise *because of* nationalisation is an example of fallacious reasoning.

(ii) *Applying something which is true of a part to the whole.* A has more money than before, and is better off. But to assume that if everyone has more money, everyone is better off may be fallacious.

8. The difficulties of economics. There are a number of difficulties in the study of economics which are not met with in the physical sciences such as chemistry or physics. They are as follows:

(a) *The economist is involved* in the subject matter of his study; he cannot therefore be objective.

(b) *Controlled experiments are virtually impossible.*

(c) *It is very difficult, if not impossible, to make measurements.* It is necessary to make measurements to make predictions and fashion suitable policies.

9. The significance of the study of economics. If we are to solve the many economic problems that arise—they are always present—and make the best use of our resources, it is necessary to know how the economic process works. It is as unlikely that we can provide suitable economic policies without a knowledge of economic theory as it is that we can repair a television set without knowing how it works.

A knowledge of economic theory alone will not suffice. Economic activity is only one aspect of man's behaviour and no acceptable solution to an economic problem can be found without taking into account the requirements of justice and morality.

PROGRESS TEST 1

[The numbers in the brackets after each question refer to the paragraphs within the chapter]

1. What part does man play in the economic process? (1)
2. What is meant by a factor of production? (1)
3. What is economics and what kind of things does an economist study? (1, 3, 7)
4. What do you understand by the economic process? (2)
5. What is production? (2)
6. How are incomes earned? Distinguish real incomes from money incomes. (2)
7. What is the relationship between factor costs and incomes? (2)
8. What is meant by (a) consumption goods, (b) capital? (2)
9. What is wealth and what relation does it bear to welfare? (3)
10. Is money a part of wealth? (3)
11. What is studied in: (a) the economics of distribution, (b) the economics of production, (c) micro-economics, (d) macro-economics? (3, 1)
12. What is an economic problem and how does it arise? (4)
13. What are the main economic problems of an individual? (4)
14. What are the main economic problems of the community? (4)
15. Distinguish between an economic problem and a technical one, illustrating by means of examples of your own. (4)
16. What is meant by (a) the private sector, (b) the public sector, of the economy? (5)

17. How does a "mixed" economy differ from either a planned economy or a *laisser-faire* economy? (5)

18. If you were responsible for the economic policy of the Government what would your main aims be? (6)

19. Why is economics (a) a social science, (b) a positive science? (7)

20. What is meant by inductive reasoning and deductive reasoning? Give examples of your own. (7)

21. How does Lord Robbins define economics? (7)

22. Give examples of your own of fallacious arguments in economics. (7)

23. What difficulties do we find in the study of economics which are not found in studying physical sciences such as physics? (8)

24. Of what use is the study of economics? (9)

CHAPTER II

THE NATIONAL INCOME

1. Social accounting. The economic process (described in Chapter I, 2; illustrated in Fig. 1) must be measured if practical policies are to be formulated upon which useful action can be taken.

The total product needs to be measured and analysed. This measuring and analysis is known as *social accounting*.

2. The national income. There are three ways of regarding the national income: as

    (i) the *total goods and services produced* in a given period,
   (ii) the *total incomes earned* in a given period,
  (iii) the *total expenditure* in a given period.

Imagine an economy to consist of six firms: a farm, a flour-mill, a bakery, a mine, an iron works, and an oven-manufacturing firm. The profit and loss accounts are as follows:

FARM

	£		£
Wages	10,000	Sales 20,000	
Profit	10,000	—wheat	
	20,000		20,000

MINE

	£		£
Wages	8,000	Sales 16,000	
Profit	8,000	—iron ore	
	16,000		16,000

FLOUR MILL

	£		£
Wheat	20,000	Sales 50,000	
Wages	15,000	—flour	
Profits	15,000		
	50,000		50,000

IRON WORKS

	£		£
Iron		Sales 36,000	
ore	16,000	—iron	
Wages	10,000		
Profit	10,000		
	36,000		36,000

BAKERY		OVEN FACTORY	
£	£	£	£
Flour 50,000	Sales 170,000	Iron 36,000	Sales 70,000
Wages 40,000	—bread	Wages 24,000	—ovens
Profit 80,000		Profit 10,000	
170,000	170,000	70,000	70,000

The farm sold its wheat to the flour mill, which turned the wheat to flour and sold it to the bakery; the bakery turned the flour into bread and sold it to the owners of the various firms and to the workers of those firms. The mine sold its output of iron ore to the iron works, which converted it to iron and sold it to the oven factory. The ovens were sold to the bakery.

The national income of our imaginary economy

(i) *as the total goods and services produced*

		£	£
Agriculture:	farm		20,000
Mining:	mine		16,000
Manufacturing:	flour mill		
	(Sales £50,000 *less* purchase of wheat, farm's output £20,000)	30,000	
	bakery		
	(Sales £170,000 *less* purchase of flour, mill's and farm's output £50,000)	120,000	
	iron works		
	(Sales £36,000 *less* purchase of iron ore, mine's output £16,000)	20,000	
	oven factory		
	(Sales £70,000 *less* purchase of iron, iron works' and mine's output £36,000)	34,000	
			204,000
			240,000

(ii) *as the total incomes earned*

		£	£
Wages:	farm workers	10,000	
	miners	8,000	
	factory workers	89,000	
	(£15,000 + £40,000 + £10,000 + £24,000)		
			107,000
Profit:	farmer	10,000	
	miller	15,000	
	baker	80,000	
	mine-owner	8,000	
	owner of iron works	10,000	
	owner of oven factory	10,000	
			133,000
			240,000

(iii) *as the total expenditure*

		£
Consumption goods:	bread	170,000
Capital goods:	ovens	70,000
		240,000

✱ In finding the total product, it would not be correct to add wheat £20,000, flour £50,000, bread £170,000, iron ore £16,000, iron £36,000, ovens £70,000, making a total of £362,000. The wheat would be counted more than once: as wheat, again as part of the flour, and yet once more as part of the bread; and the iron would also be counted more than once. This fault is known as *double counting*. To avoid it, all goods and services bought from other firms, that is, outputs of other firms, must be deducted to get the output of any particular firm.

It will be seen that the value of the total goods and services produced is the same as the total factor costs (Chapter I, 2) and these are incomes. *Real income* consists of the goods and services obtained from money income and this must therefore be the same as the total product. Expenditure consisting of (i) expenditure on consumption goods and (ii) expenditure on capital goods must also be the same as the product (compare with flow diagram, Chapter I, 2).

TABLE 1. U.K. NATIONAL INCOME, 1973

(i) *National product at factor cost*

	£ million
Agriculture, forestry, fishing, mining and quarrying	2,744
Manufacturing, construction, gas, electricity and water	25,471
Transport and communications	5,460
Distribution trades, insurance, banking, and finance and other service	20,509
Public administration and defence, public health and education	7,992
Net property income from abroad	1,095
	63,271

(ii) *National income*

	£ million
Incomes from work (wages, salaries)	49,134
Incomes from businesses and property (profits, interests, rents, dividends)	14,137
	63,271

(iii) *National expenditure*

	£ million
Expenditure on consumption goods and services	58,125
Expenditure on capital goods	13,696
	71,821
less expenditure taxes (*less* subsidies) included in above	8,550
	63,271

3. Gross and net national income. In earning the national income, *i.e.* producing the national product, existing capital is used up. This is what accountants call depreciation. The economist refers to it as *capital consumption*.

A year's use of all capital goods used in producing a year's national product (*i.e.* the capital consumption for the year), must be deducted from the *gross national income* (at total factor cost) to arrive at the *net national income* for the year.

GROSS NATIONAL INCOME *less* **CAPITAL** = **NET NATIONAL**
AT FACTOR COST   **CONSUMPTION**   **INCOME**

> U.K. national income, 1973
>
> | *Gross national* | *Capital* | *National* |
> | income | consumption | income |
> | £63,271m. | *less* £7,012m. | =£56,259m. |

It is impossible to give an accurate figure for capital consumption—the life of capital goods such as plant and machinery is not known. However, Government statisticians give an estimate, based mainly on income tax depreciation allowances.

NOTE:

(a) When referring to the national income, unless the context suggests otherwise, it is the *net* national income that is meant.

(b) When it is a question of analysing the national income into its various components it is always the gross national income or gross national product or gross national expenditure that is analysed.

* Remember that the gross national product, the gross national income, and the gross national expenditure are the *same* thing, but looked at from different points of view.

4. The components of the national income. Part of the national income earned by *residents* in this country is derived from property which is located abroad; *e.g.* they may own shares in a foreign company. Income is also earned in the form of interest on loans made to people residing abroad.

On the other hand *non-residents* may own property in this country from which they too can earn an income. They also make loans to people in this country and earn interest.

NOTE:

(a) The income earned from abroad less the income payable abroad may be termed *net income from abroad*.

(b) The difference between the gross national income and the net income from abroad is known as the *gross domestic product*.

(c) The gross domestic product is the total goods and services produced in a country in a given period.

GROSS NATIONAL INCOME (OR GROSS NATIONAL PRODUCT)	=	NET INCOME FROM ABROAD	+	GROSS DOMESTIC PRODUCT

U.K. national income, 1973

Gross national product		Net income from abroad		Gross domestic product
£63,271m.	=	£1,095m.	+	£62,176m.

(d) *Expenditure taxes* (Chapter XXI) are those taxes such as value added tax and import duties added to the selling price.

The total taxes going to the Government from this source are equal to the increase in selling prices. The Government has additional income corresponding to the additional prices.

Expenditure taxes do not add to the national income, but do add to the money value of it when expressed at market prices instead of at factor cost.

(e) *Subsidies* are the exact opposite of an expenditure tax; they are payments made by the Government and are deducted from the selling price at factor cost.

GROSS NATIONAL EXPENDITURE AT FACTOR COST	+	EXPENDITURE TAXES (*less* SUBSIDIES)	=	GROSS NATIONAL EXPENDITURE AT MARKET PRICES

U.K. national income, 1973

Gross national expenditure at factor cost		Expenditure taxes (*less subsidies*)		Gross national expenditure at market prices
£63, 271m.	+	£8,550m.	=	£71,821m.

(f) The *gross national expenditure* can be analysed into:

(i) *Expenditure on consumption goods* and
(ii) *Investment*, which in this context means additions to real capital: *see* 12 *below*.

GROSS NATIONAL EXPENDITURE AT MARKET PRICES	=	EXPENDITURE ON CONSUMPTION GOODS AT MARKET PRICES	+	INVESTMENT AT MARKET PRICES

U.K. national income, 1973.

Gross national expenditure at market prices		Expenditure on consumption goods at market prices		Investment at market prices
£71,821m.	=	£58,125m.	+	£13,696m.

(g) The *gross national expenditure* can also be analysed into:

    (i) *Gross domestic expenditure*, and

    (ii) *Investment (or dis-investment) abroad*.

GROSS NATIONAL EXPENDITURE AT MARKET PRICES	=	GROSS DOMESTIC EXPENDITURE AT MARKET PRICES	+ INVESTMENT ABROAD *or* − DIS-INVESTMENT ABROAD

U.K. National income, 1973

Gross national expenditure at market prices		*Gross domestic expenditure at market prices*	*Dis-investment abroad*
£71,821m.	=	£72,570m.	− £749m.

Investment abroad is that part of the gross national expenditure which is not spent in this country. The part which is so spent is the *gross domestic expenditure*. The amount of investment abroad is obtained by deducting from exports and property income received from abroad imports and property income paid abroad.

Dis-investment abroad arises where imports and property income paid abroad exceeds exports and property income received from abroad. Gross domestic expenditure will exceed gross national expenditure. Spending has exceeded income.

During 1973 grants abroad (*i.e.* gifts) amounted to £461m. As this amount is not included in the gross domestic expenditure, it should be added to the figure of £749m. given as dis-investment abroad to give the real figure of £1,210m. which then agrees with the deficit balance on current account of the Balance of Payments (Chapter XIX).

(h) *Gross domestic expenditure* can be analysed into:

    (i) *Domestic capital formation* (*i.e.* increase in investment at home) and

    (ii) *Consumption*.

GROSS DOMESTIC EXPENDITURE AT MARKET PRICES	=	DOMESTIC CAPITAL FORMATION	+ CONSUMPTION

U.K. National income, 1973

Gross domestic expenditure at market prices		*Domestic capital formation*	*Consumption*
£72,570m.	=	£14,445m.	+ £58,125m.

The relationship between the various components of the national income is shown in Fig. 2. Compare the equations given above with this diagram.

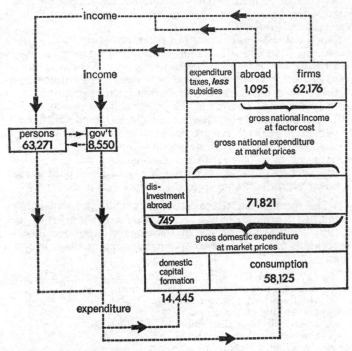

NOTE: The figures refer to the year 1973 in £million

FIG. 2.—*National income and expenditure flows.*

5. Transfer payments. Incomes in the form of wages and profits are *factor costs*.

Incomes may also be in the form of social security payments such as unemployment benefit, children's allowances, and old age pensions. These incomes are known as *transfer payments* and are incomes transferred from one set of persons to another by way of income tax.

Such incomes, which are not factor costs, are *not part of the national income*.

6. National Debt interest. The Government of Great Britain borrows money by issuing stocks (*e.g.* Consols, war bonds). The total amount owed by the Government in respect of money borrowed is known as the *National Debt*: Chapter XXI. Interest payable by the Government on this National Debt is *National Debt interest*.

Nearly all the Debt is owed to people residing in this country; *i.e.* it is nearly all *internal debt*. Furthermore, the Debt is, for the most part, not represented by any assets, the money borrowed being spent mainly on past wars. The interest paid on this debt is not part of the cost of anything produced; it is not a factor cost. It is a *transfer payment*, the interest paid to one set of persons from income tax collected from another set. A person may well receive interest from his Government stocks and at the same time pay income tax. Such transfer payments cannot be part of the national income.

Any part of the interest on the National Debt paid abroad is, however, a deduction from the national income.

7. The compilation of the National Income and Expenditure Accounts. These accounts are published each year by the Central Statistical Office. An extremely large number of sources are used in their compilation. Among these may be listed:

    (i) the Inland Revenue, the main source for compiling the national income as a total of incomes,
   (ii) the Census of Production,
  (iii) the Census of Distribution,
  (iv) the accounts of the nationalised industries,
   (v) the Government accounts,
  (vi) the Family Expenditure Survey
 (vii) the Department of Trade's statistics of retail sales.

Items (ii) to (v) provide the main sources for compiling the national product. Items (v)—the Government is responsible for about one third of the national expenditure—(vi), and (vii) are some of the sources used to compile the national expenditure.

It will be appreciated that many goods produced and services rendered do not enter into the market and yet are part of the national income. Among these are:

   (a) *Goods consumed by those who produce them.* These are included where practicable, *e.g.* in the case of farmers.

(b) *Unpaid personal services.* Despite their magnitude, particularly those rendered by housewives, they must be omitted as it is not practicable to include them.

(c) *"Free" Government services.* These include such things as education and the health services. Since salaries are paid to teachers and Government servants, these will be included in the national income.

(d) *Service given by houses occupied by owners.* If a person rents a house, the rent received by the owner is part of the owner's income (received for the use of his property) and the rent paid by the occupier is part of the occupier's expenditure. Such rent is part of the national income.

When a house is occupied by the owner the rental value (the amount of rent he could get if he let it) must be included in the national income.

8. The determinants of the level of the national income.

(a) *The natural resources available.* Raw materials—crude oil, coal, iron, wood, wheat, etc.—are the basic requirements of production: *see* Chapter III.

(b) *The amount of capital equipment.* Resources that are not obtainable are useless. Many countries such as Brazil are poor because their rich natural resources cannot yet be exploited for lack of the necessary equipment.

(c) *Technical knowledge.* In order to make the greatest use of natural resources, knowledge is required. The use of tides to produce power, breeding fish instead of "hunting" them, the production of man-made fibres, all these things have only become possible with recently acquired knowledge.

(d) *The number and quality of the working population.* A healthy, intelligent people will produce more than a sickly, ignorant population (for the effect of size of population on production, *see* Chapter VI, 4).

(e) *Government action and direction.* Acts of Parliament and Government regulations may encourage or discourage production (for the effect of taxation upon economic incentive, *see* Chapter XXI, 7).

The Government can influence the level of employment and hence the national income by its monetary and fiscal policies: *see* Chapters XXI, XXII, *and* XXIII.

9. The national income and the standard of living. The national income is the money expression of a total of goods and services. More goods and services per person would seem to indicate a higher standard of living, by material standards at least. But a good deal of what is produced depends upon political conditions and environment. Thus, in many countries, a large part of the national income consists of defence materials and transport services. Much of what is produced, although necessary, might well not add to the standard of living.

10. Comparison of the national incomes of different countries. Great care is needed in comparing the national incomes of different countries if valid conclusions are to be drawn. Attention should be paid to the following points:

(a) *Differences in population.* It will be necessary to divide the national incomes by the respective populations.

(b) *Differences in price levels.* Incomes may be greater in one country than in another, but prices may also be higher.

(c) *Differences in conditions.* People in warm countries need less fuel; some countries need protection against floods.

(d) *Differences in the amount of production entering the market.* More housewives may go out to work in one country than in another. More of the population may be self-supporting in one country than in another.

(e) *Differences in costs of production.* The national income may be inflated by costs of transport necessary in one country but not in another.

(f) *Differences in what is produced* The goods and services produced will vary in kind from one country to another.

11. Comparison of the national income of one year with that of another. In comparing the national income of a country over the years, allowances must be made for:

(a) *Changing population.* Twice the national income for twice the population means no increase in income per person.

(b) *Changing prices.* If the national income has doubled but prices have also doubled, there is no *real* increase in production. In the Blue book, the national income is given not only at current prices, but also for a number of years at the prices of a particular year.

(c) *Changing types of goods and services.* Examples are the use of electricity instead of gas for lighting, motor cars instead of horse-drawn carriages, plastic goods replacing those made of wood, china, etc., television replacing the music hall.

12. National income and national wealth. The national income consists of goods and services produced in a year. Of these, a part will be consumed. This will be the consumption goods and services *actually* bought by consumers. The remainder will consist of capital goods and unsold stocks. These are additions to the capital existing at the beginning of the year and are known as *investment*. This investment is an addition to the national wealth: Chapter I, 3.

13. The uses of national income statistics. The data available, showing what a country has produced, the extent of its investment, the distribution of incomes, and the economic transactions of the Government, provide a basis upon which a government can plan its economic policy. The Government is enabled to know the possibilities of production, to what extent it can be increased and in what directions it may be changed.

PROGRESS TEST 2

1. What is meant by social accounting and what are its uses? (1, 13)

2. How is double counting avoided in compiling the national product? (2)

3. There are three ways of regarding the national income. What are they? (2)

4. What do you understand by the national income and how can it be measured? (2, 3)

5. Distinguish between national income and national wealth. (Chapter I, 3, Chapter II, 12)

6. What is the relationship between consumption, investment, and gross national expenditure? (4)

(7) What is the relationship between gross national income at factor cost and gross national expenditure at market prices? (4)

8. What is meant by the gross domestic product and how does it vary from the gross national product? (4)

9. What is a transfer payment? Is it part of the national income? (5)

10. Is National Debt interest a transfer payment? (6)

11. How would you deal with the following in compiling the national income: (a) farm produce consumed by the farmer; (b) owner occupied dwellings; (c) Government services for which no charge is made; (d) unpaid personal services such as those rendered by a housewife?

Give reasons for your treatment. (7)

12. What are the main factors which determine the level of the national product and how can it be ncreased? (8)

13. To what extent, is the national income indicative of the standard of living of a country? (9)

14. What precautions are necessary when comparing the national incomes of two different countries? (10)

15. If you were comparing the national income of this country for last year with that of twenty years ago, what points would you bear in mind to ensure that your conclusions were valid? (11)

16.

	£ million
Gross domestic product at factor cost	39,580
Transfer payments and national debt interest	4,620
Expenditure taxes (less subsidies)	4,580
Net income from abroad	747
Capital consumption	3,145
Exports	682
Imports	714
Expenditure on consumption goods and services	36,512

From the above hypothetical data calculate:

(a) Gross national product at factor cost,

(b) National income,

(c) Gross national product at market prices,

(d) Gross domestic expenditure at market prices,

(e) Domestic capital formation at market prices,

(f) Net investment abroad.

(4, Fig. 2)

Solution. This has been printed upside down so that you do not refer to it before attempting the question.

		£ million
Gross domestic product at factor cost		39,580
add net income from abroad		747
(a) Gross national income at factor cost		40,327
less capital consumption		3,145
(b) National income		37,182
Gross national income at factor cost		40,327
add expenditure taxes (less subsidies)		4,580
(c) Gross national product at market prices		44,907
less net investment abroad		715
(d) Gross domestic expenditure at market prices		44,192
less expenditure on consumption goods and services		36,512
(e) Domestic capital formation at market prices		7,680
(f) Net investment abroad (747+682−714)		715

CHAPTER III

PRODUCTION

1. Nature of production. Production consists of using resources in order to obtain goods and services. Resources are taken and combined in such a way that *utilities* are created.

(a) *Production as the creation of utilities.*

(i) *Changing the form of materials* (utility of form). Iron ore becomes steel, wood is made into furniture.
(ii) *Changing the place of commodities* (utility of place), *e.g.* transporting cocoa from Ghana to Britain.
(iii) *Storing goods until required* (utility of time). This entails the use of resources (warehouses, labour of storekeepers) and hence is production.
(iv) *Providing a service* (utilities of time, place, or form). Resources are used, *e.g.* in the case of a haircut, clippers among other things, the hairdresser's labour, and the premises where the operation takes place. It is left to the reader to say what utilities are created.

* A service is consumed as soon as it is produced, whereas a commodity is consumed some time *after* production. Usually, a commodity gives a number of services; for example, a motor car can be used over a number of years. A commodity has been defined as a "bundle" of services.

* Utility does not mean "usefulness." In economics, it is the quality of being wanted. Thus "utility of form" means the form wanted.

(b) *Production as the creation of value.* Every time any resources are used, the suppliers will be paid. The value (Chapter I, 3) of the product increases by a corresponding amount. Hence, production may be defined as the creation of value.

2. Factors of production. These are the resources used in production. The many thousands of different factors of production may be classified into:

(a) *Capital, i.e.* property of all kinds—buildings, machines, materials—used in production,

(b) *Labour, i.e.* work of any kind (human effort expended to earn an income). It includes management. To an economist, the managing director, as well as the sweeper on the shop floor, provides labour.

It is often useful to distinguish between certain kinds of capital as it is sometimes useful to distinguish between certain kinds of labour. Hence, most economists would separate land from capital.

(c) *Land* includes not only land itself but all other gifts of nature, *e.g.* soil and mineral deposits. It is the ultimate source of all materials and natural forces and provides space where production can be carried out.

TABLE 2. INCOMES FROM FACTORS OF PRODUCTION

Factor of production	Income received by owner of factor	
Capital	Interest (for its use)	(Chapter XII)
	Profit (for risk that it may be lost)	(Chapter XIII)
Labour	Wages	(Chapter XI)
Land	Commercial rent	(Chapter XIV)

Substitution of factors of production. It is possible to replace one factor of production by another when combining factors, *e.g.* machines may replace labour. But it is not possible to do so completely. *Any factor of production which cannot be completely substituted for another constitutes a separate factor of production.*

Factors of production are measured in physical units, *e.g.* acres of land, so many machines, man-hours of work, units of electricity, etc. They can also be measured in terms of cost: Chapter IX.

* Do not confuse the factor of production itself with the owner of the factor. It is possible for a person to provide both capital and labour, *e.g.* the ironmasters and the mill owners of the nineteenth century. Their work consisted in running their own businesses.

3. The entrepreneur. This term is used to mean either

(a) *the owner of a business,* or

(b) *the man who manages the business, i.e.* co-ordinates the factors of production.

Where one man combines both functions no difficulty arises. However, the owners of a business are not always the people who manage it. The entrepreneurs are now usually taken to mean the *owners* of a business, that is, the people who supply the capital and run the risk of losing it.

On the other hand, the entrepreneurial function refers to control, management, and co-ordination. This is, in fact, a particular kind of labour.

* The entrepreneur who owned a business (provided capital) *and* also managed it (provided labour), according to the older textbooks, provided *enterprise*, which was treated as a fourth factor of production. This is *not* the current practice.

4. The law of diminishing marginal productivity. This law is more commonly known as the *law of diminishing returns*. It is also known as the law of non-proportional returns and the law of variable proportions.

The law of diminishing marginal productivity states that: *if increasing quantities of one factor of production are used in conjunction with a fixed quantity of other factors, then, after a certain point, each successive unit of the variable factor will make a smaller and smaller addition to the total output.*

This law must be true because, if it were not, it would for example be possible to grow all the potatoes required for the whole world by setting more and more men to work on one field or, alternatively, giving one man more and more ground. The whole world's requirements for any particular manufactured commodity could be obtained from one small factory by employing more and more men or, alternatively, giving one man more and more factories.

The law shows the *relationship* between *the amount of resources* used in physical terms (*e.g.* tons of iron ore, coal; man-hours, etc.) and *the amount of output* in physical terms (*e.g.* tons of iron).

It relates to a given period of time, with a given state of technical knowledge.

The *units* of the variable factor are of equal efficiency; diminishing returns arise because they are being used less efficiently.

In Table 3 imaginary data are given to illustrate the law. The area of land cultivated, the quantity of seed potatoes available, the amount of equipment, in fact every factor of production is fixed in quantity *except* the number of men employed for the season. Thus, if one man were employed, the total output would be 6 tons of potatoes. If two men were employed instead of one the total output would be 18 tons, and so on. Two men working together, if equally efficient workers, will usually produce more than twice as much as one man working on his own. As the number of men employed increases, output increases more than proportionately *up to a point*. Then, after a certain point is reached, the average output per man decreases—in our illustration, after the third man.

TABLE 3. LAW OF DIMINISHING MARGINAL PRODUCTIVITY

	Units of variable factor	*Total product*	*Marginal product*	*Average product*
	(*men*)	(*tons*)	(*tons*)	(*tons*)
Phase One	0	0	0	0
	1	6	6	6
	2	18	12	9
	3	33	15	11
Phase Two	4	40	7	10
	5	45	5	9
	6	48	3	8
	7	49	1	7
Phase Three	8	40	—9	5

NOTE:

(i) The *marginal product* is the additional product obtained from combining one more unit of the variable factor. Thus, total product when two men are employed is 18 tons; when three men are employed it is 33 tons. The additional product, employing one more man, is $33 - 18 = 15$ tons. The marginal product is 15 tons.

(ii) The *average product* per unit of variable factor is obtained by dividing the total product by the number of units of the variable factor employed. Thus, when three men are employed the average product per man (the variable factor in our illustration) is 33 tons divided by 3, *i.e.* 11 tons per man.

The three phases of the law can best be distinguished by studying Fig. 3, where the data given in Table 3 are shown in the form of a graph.

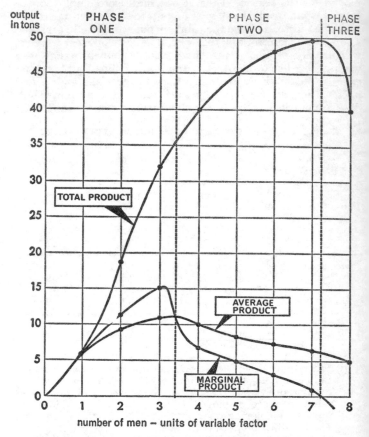

FIG. 3.—*The law of diminishing marginal productivity.*
NOTE: Neither the point where average product = marginal product (at the point of highest average product) nor the point of highest total product coincide with any observations (*i.e.* figures given in the data).

Phase One: average product per unit of variable factor is increasing. The phase ends at the point where the average product is highest and at this point it is equal to the marginal product.

Phase Two: the average product is decreasing during this phase, which ends at the point where total product is highest and marginal product is zero. Total product is still increasing during this phase.

Phase Three: total product is decreasing, average product continues to decrease, and marginal product is negative.

* NOTE: (i) the marginal product curve cuts the average product curve at the point of highest average product, (ii) the marginal product curve cuts the x axis when the total product is at its highest point, (iii) the marginal product starts to fall before the average product falls.

5. The "lowest cost" combination of factors. It is not possible to state from the law of diminishing marginal productivity how many units of the variable factor should be combined with the fixed factors in order to give the lowest cost per unit of output. It is necessary to know the *cost* of the factors.

Suppose that the *fixed factors are free* but that the variable factor must be paid for. Then, in order to get the lowest cost per unit of output, the number of units of the variable factor which would be used would be that which gave the highest average product, indicated on the diagram at the beginning of Phase Two.

If, on the other hand, the *variable factor is free*, but fixed factors have to be paid for, then the number of units of the variable factor employed would be at the point where marginal product was nil, indicated on the diagram at the end of Phase Two.

However, since both variable and fixed factors have to be paid for, it follows that the number of units of the variable factor employed will be somewhere in Phase Two, depending upon the relative costs of the fixed and the variable factors: *see* Chapter IX.

* A very frequent error is to state that additions of the variable factor will be made until the point of diminishing returns is reached. As can be seen from the diagram both marginal *and* average returns are diminishing throughout the whole of Phase Two.

6. Specialisation. A man specialises in doing a particular job or process. Capital equipment is specialised for use in one particular operation. Land is also specialised, certain land being used for building, other land for pasture, and so on.

Specialisation means greater output from any given resources: *see 7 below.* It gives rise to large-scale production and its consequent economies (Chapter IV) and hence to a higher standard of living.

7. The law of comparative advantage. Specialisation not in accordance with the *law of comparative advantage* (also known as the *law of comparative costs*) will not increase output. This law states that: *if any factor of production is employed in that use in which it has the greatest comparative advantage or the least comparative disadvantage, output is maximised.*

As an illustration of this law, consider two men, A and B, and compare the total product when they specialise with the total product when they do not specialise.

A can produce in 8 hours either 4 chairs *or* 100 loaves. B can produce in 8 hours either 6 chairs *or* 120 loaves.

TABLE 4. LAW OF COMPARATIVE ADVANTAGE

	Chairs		Loaves
Without specialisation			
(devoting 4 hours to each commodity)			
A produces	2	*plus*	50
B produces	3	*plus*	60
Total product	5	*plus*	110
With specialisation			
(in accordance with the law, each devoting 8 hours to one commodity)			
A produces	—		100
B produces	6		—
Total product	6	*plus*	100
Gains from specialisation:	1	*less*	10

B, it is noted, can produce more of either commodity. He has an absolute advantage in the production of both commodities over A. But whereas he produces $1\frac{1}{2}$ times as many chairs, he only produces $1\frac{1}{5}$ times as many loaves with the same amount of labour. He has the greater comparative advantage in producing chairs.

A, on the other hand, produces $\frac{5}{6}$ as many loaves as B but only $\frac{4}{6}$ as many chairs. He has the lesser comparative disadvantage in producing loaves.

Therefore to gain from specialisation, B must produce chairs and A must produce loaves.

For A the value of 1 chair is 25 loaves (both cost him 2 hours' labour). At A's valuation the gains from specialisation amount to 15 loaves. For B the value of 1 chair is 20 loaves (both cost him $1\frac{1}{3}$ hours). At B's valuation the gains from specialisation amount to 10 loaves.

Terms of trade: A will exchange loaves for chairs from B. The rate of exchange will be between 20 and 25 loaves for 1 chair.

Specialisation has necessitated exchange; otherwise each specialist has only one product or part of a product and lacks others which he needs. Specialisation and exchange mean that everyone is better off.

* Notice in the illustration that the ratios $1\frac{1}{2}$ times as many chairs and $1\frac{1}{5}$ times as many loaves are different. Had they been the same, there could have been no gains from specialisation.

8. The division of labour. This is the specialisation of labour into jobs, processes, or even parts of a process.

(a) *The advantages* may be summed up as follows:

  (i) *Economy of labour.* Specialisation of labour in accordance with the law of comparative costs means a greater output for a given amount of labour.

  (ii) *Economy of time.* Time is saved (*a*) in learning how to do the job; often only one particular machine operation has to be known (*b*) because skill is acquired by always doing one particular job (*c*) because no time is lost in changing from one task to another.

  (iii) *Economy of capital.* Fewer tools and less equipment are required. Moreover they are used continuously.

(b) *The disadvantages* usually associated with the division of labour are as follows:

    (i) *Monotony of work.* But routine work is often suitable for certain types of worker.

    (ii) *Risk of unemployment* if a worker is very specialised.

    (iii) *Standardised products.* But standardisation has many advantages (lower cost, ease of obtaining replacements) and an "individual" product can nearly always be bought instead, although at a higher price.

    ✻ The aim of specialisation is *not* to give people the job they can do best but the one in which they are most productive.

(c) *The limitations* to the division of labour are:

    (i) *The extent of the market.* A commodity for which there is little demand offers little scope for extensive specialisation of labour. Transport facilities play a great part in delimiting the market.

    (ii) *Technical possibilities.* After a certain point it is not possible to divide a process further.

PROGRESS TEST 3

1. What does an economist understand by production? Would you include a cabaret show as production? (1)

2. What is a factor of production? How would you distinguish one factor from another? (2)

3. Define (a) land, (b) capital, (c) labour, (d) entrepreneur. (2, 3)

4. State the law of diminishing marginal productivity. Is it always true? (4)

5. What is meant by the average product per unit of variable resource? Give a numerical example. (4)

6. What is meant by the marginal product? Give a numerical example. (4)

7. What are the three phases of the law of diminishing marginal productivity? (4)

8. In order to find the best combination of the factors of production, additions of the variable factor will be made until the point of diminishing returns is reached. Do you agree? If not, state why, and say how the lowest cost combination is reached. (5)

9. What is meant by specialisation and what are its advantages? (6)

10. State the law of comparative advantage. What is its importance? **(7)**

11. What do you understand by the terms of trade? Give a numerical example. **(7)**

12. What is meant by the division of labour? **(8)**

13. What advantages are obtained from the division of labour? **(8)**

14. The division of labour entails certain disadvantages. What are they? **(8)**

15. What are the limitations to the division of labour? **(8)**

CHAPTER IV

THE STRUCTURE OF INDUSTRY

1. Firm and industry.

(a) *A production unit* is an establishment where production is carried out, *e.g.* a factory, a shop, or a farm.

(b) *A firm* usually refers to one or more production units having the same ownership.

(c) *An industry* consists of a number of firms engaged in producing a commodity for the same market. However, to quote E. A. G. Robinson (*The Structure of Competitive Industry*), "to define it by the commodity produced or by the market for which it produces, is in many cases either impossible or at least unsatisfactory. In practice, all we can do is to follow the example of those who are actually engaged in industries. Certain employers find they have a common bond of interest with certain other employers, and come to regard themselves as composing an industry. The bond may be one of the broad type of general product as in the motor industry . . . it may be the common use of a single raw material as in the iron and steel industry . . . the common use of a given type of machinery, or of a given process of manufacture."

A firm may so diversify its products that it belongs to many industries.

A production unit can also be owned by more than one firm.

2. Economies of scale.
As a firm grows bigger, that is, increases its output, its cost of production per unit of output can fall; it achieves economies of growth. The reasons for this are:

(i) *Increasing scope for the division of labour and the specialisation of machines.*

(ii) *The principle of large machines.* Larger machines and equipment cost proportionally less than smaller ones to buy and maintain, and require proportionally fewer workers to use them. A six-ton lorry does not require two drivers because a three-ton lorry requires one.

(iii) *The principle of the least common multiple.* Production
will consist of many processes, each of which will require
equipment which is only obtainable in certain sizes,
capable of dealing with certain outputs, in a given time.
The capacities of these machines and plant will vary
from process to process. As the output of a firm becomes
larger there is less likelihood of machines and equipment
being only partly used.

Suppose the production of a certain commodity requires
only two processes. Suppose, further, that the only equipment available for the first process can deal with 12 units
of output per day and that the only equipment available
for the second process can deal with 15 units per day.
Then, the smallest output per day which entails the
machines being fully used is 60 units—L.C.M. of 12 and 15.

(iv) *The principle of massed reserves.* Stocks of all kinds are
required, materials in the factory, stationery in the office,
and finished goods in the warehouse. The stocks required
do not grow in the same proportion as the growth of the
firm. The extension of branch banking has enabled banks
to hold a smaller proportion of their deposits in the form of
till money.

Economies which arise from the growth of a firm are known
as *internal economies.* They may be classified as:

(i) *Technical economies.* These refer to the savings effected in
the actual making in the factory or works. Technical
economies usually continue indefinitely.

(ii) *Managerial economies.* These refer to savings effected in the
administration of the business. Here, again, they arise
through the increased scope of the division of labour, and
in so far as the office is mechanised the principle of large
machines will apply. But as a firm becomes larger so do the
difficulties of co-ordination; hence, beyond a certain size,
diseconomies will be experienced—the cost of management
will rise because of the necessity of complicated and costly
methods of effective co-ordination.

(iii) *Financial economies.* The larger firm can usually raise
capital more cheaply than a small one. Investors have
greater confidence in a large firm whose shares are quoted
on the stock exchange. Large firms can offer better
security to bankers.

(iv) *Marketing economies.* Buying in large quantities means
lower prices. Where a firm is large enough to take a big
proportion of the total supply, it may obtain low prices by
its favourable bargaining position.

In selling, a large firm can effect considerable economies. Larger sales do not entail proportionately higher costs in invoicing, packing, advertising, salesmen's salaries. Moreover, where a firm sells more than one product, they advertise each other.

However, after a certain point, diseconomies arise. To sell increased output more intensive advertising is required; after-sales service must be given; longer credit, "free" gifts, and other expensive sales promotion methods used; exporting (with increased transport costs, more expensive packing, and special advertising suitable for overseas markets) becomes necessary.

(v) *Risk-bearing economies.* The small firm is at no great disadvantage in insuring against insurable risks. However, for those risks against which a firm does not insure, preferring to bear the risks in order to increase profits, the larger the firm the less the risk of loss. In fact, if a firm is large enough, it pays it to be its own insurer.

The risk of loss arising from changes in demand (which cannot be insured against) is less for a large firm which can diversify its output or its markets. Risks from the supply side can be avoided by diversification of sources and production methods.

3. The optimum size firm. This has been defined as *"that firm which in existing conditions of technique and organising ability has the lowest average cost of production per unit when all those costs which must be covered in the long run are included"* (E. A. G. Robinson).

The cost of production can be divided into manufacturing costs (technical), administrative costs (managerial), selling costs (marketing), etc. The technical optimum (the size which gives the lowest average technical cost per unit), the marketing optimum, the managerial optimum, and the financial optimum are unlikely to be the same. It follows, since all costs have to be met and a firm cannot be a different size for each type of cost, that there can be more than one optimum size firm, that is, more than one firm can have the lowest average cost per unit of output.

The growth of firms is dependent upon the availability of capital. For this reason firms may not grow to their optimum size. Again, the entrepreneur may be more interested in ruling a large "empire" than in efficiency, and a firm may be larger than the optimum size.

4. The predominance of the small firm. Although a large firm means lower costs, the small firm has survived; indeed the vast majority of firms are small. There are many reasons for this:

(a) *The demand is small.* Examples are where the commodity or service offered is of limited appeal, and when the market is small (for example, the village bakery). A market may be small because transport costs limit it geographically.

(b) *No large-scale economies possible.* (i) Personal services, *e.g.* hair-dressing, domestic help. (ii) Production of goods in accordance with individual requirements, *e.g.* exclusive models of dresses.

(c) *Lack of capital.* The accumulation of capital leading to economic growth is a slow process.

(d) *Desire to be self-employed.* Even though the owner could earn more as an employee, by exploiting himself—and often his family as well—the firm continues to exist. However, the mortality rate of such firms is high.

(e) *Imperfect competition.* Product differentiation (often no more than a "brand" name, backed up by "publicity" advertising) splits the market for a commodity into a number of small markets for "different" commodities.

(f) *Toleration by large firms.* It is often not worth while for a large firm to drive a small "competitor" out of business. Furthermore, the large firm can then show that it is not a monopolist.

(g) *Co-operation with other small firms.* Small farms share capital equipment and own their "marketing department" jointly (farmers' co-operatives). Small retail grocers co-operate through wholesalers and share managerial and marketing services (*e.g.* advertising which a single small firm could not afford).

(h) *Little capital needed.* Examples include repair shops, decorators, cafés. The mortality rate of such small firms is very high.

5. Returns to scale. A firm can operate at many levels of production; it may be a small firm with comparatively little plant or, alternatively, it may be a large firm with extensive plant. In all cases, irrespective of its size, it has the problem of combining its factors of production in the most economical way. For any given scale of operations certain factors will be fixed and the law of diminishing marginal productivity will apply. This is a "short-run" law.

If the firm changes its scale of operations, *all* the factors of production will be altered. At the new level certain factors of production will again be fixed and again the law of diminishing marginal productivity will apply.

The *law of returns to scale* may be formulated thus: *if, given a certain combination of factors of production producing a given output, all the factors are increased in the same proportion and the output increases in the same proportion, returns to scale are constant. If output increases more than proportionately, there are increasing returns to scale; and if the output increases less than proportionately, there are decreasing returns to scale.*

* The law of diminishing marginal productivity refers to the effect on output when *some* factors are fixed; the law of returns to scale refers to the effect on output when *none* of the factors are fixed.

* Large scale production and standardisation are not necessarily associated. Shipbuilding is an example of large-scale production where there is no standardisation. The making of screws, which are a standardised product, can be carried out in a small workshop.

6. Integration. This refers to the amalgamation of firms with the object of lowering costs.

(a) *Vertical integration:* the amalgamation of firms engaged in *different stages* of production. In this way the source of raw materials and/or an outlet for the products can be ensured. An example is a modern steel works. It will produce the iron in blast furnaces; the iron is converted into steel in converters; it is then transferred to the rolling mill where certain steel products are made.

(b) *Horizontal integration:* the amalgamation of firms engaged in the *same stage* of production. This is usually at the marketing stage, when it is often described as a "cartel."

(c) *Lateral integration:* the amalgamation of firms engaged in producing things which can be conveniently produced simultaneously, *e.g.* clocks, speedometers, and other measuring instruments. In this way technical costs are reduced and insurance is provided against the fall in demand of one particular commodity.

7. External economics. As more firms enter an industry—that is, as the industry grows—so each firm composing that industry finds it possible to lower its costs. These economies which arise through the growth of the industry are external economics. They come about for the following reasons:

(a) *Increased specialisation.* A firm can specialise in either a particular type of commodity or in a particular process.

(b) *Better quality labour supply.* When industry is localised technical colleges can provide special courses.

(c) *Ancillary services become available*, *e.g.* organised markets, research establishments, trade journals.

(d) *Subsidiary industries* arise which provide for the main industry, *e.g.* textile machinery for the cotton and woollen industries.

Vertical disintegration, that is, ceasing to engage in certain processes or stages of production, gives rise to subsidiary industries, *e.g.* instruments are produced for motor car manufacturers by outside firms.

Firms come into existence to deal with waste materials and by-products.

✱ Do not confuse *internal* economies which arise with the growth of the firm, with *external* economies which arise from the growth of the industry.

8. Location of industry. A large number of factors determine where an industry is situated. The costs of production often vary with the location of a firm, in particular the costs of transport. There is therefore an economic and an uneconomic distribution of industry. The following are some of the factors which determine this "territorial division of labour."

(a) *Geographical determinants.* Mineral deposits, climatic and soil conditions dictate where certain commodities are to be produced.

(b) *Proximity to raw materials.* Transport costs make this particularly important where the weight of raw materials is more than the weight of the finished product (the weight of iron ore + weight of coal + weight of limestone is considerably more than the weight of iron produced).

(c) *Nearness to market.* Bulky materials are expensive to transport and may, therefore, be produced near the market. This is particularly likely where transport costs are high in relation to other costs, *e.g.* bricks.

(d) *Advantages of integration.* Different processes can be carried on in the same works, *e.g.* the manufacture of steel where iron is produced saves fuel.

(e) *Proximity to suitable labour.*

(f) *Proximity to power.* The use of electric power has in many cases diminished the importance of this factor.

(g) *Nearness to water supply.* This is of importance in a number of industries, *e.g.* many chemical industries.

(h) *Historical accident.* A number of industries are located where they are for historical reasons. The motor works at Cowley are there because Lord Nuffield began his business with a bicycle repair shop there.

(i) *Distribution of population* determines the location of shops and service trades.

(j) *Geographical inertia.* Once an industry has established itself in an area it tends to stay there even when the reasons for it doing so are no longer valid.

(k) *Attractiveness of location.* People, including directors, have to live where their work is located. This explains part at least of the pull of the south of England.

(l) *Government intervention.* This might occur where private costs and social costs differ to such an extent that without such intervention there would be an uneconomic distribution of industry.

✱ *Private costs* are those borne by the producer. *Social costs* are the total costs incurred and include, in addition to the costs borne by the producer, those borne by the community which have been caused by the acts of the producer in the course of production, *e.g.* air and water pollution.

Government policy also requires industries to be located in places where there is considerable local unemployment (*Local Employment Acts* (1960–1972).

(m) *Attraction to industrial concentrations.* Firms are attracted to where the industry of which they are a part is located in order to avail themselves of external economies (*see* **7** *above*).

Some industries can be located anywhere. An example of such a "foot-loose" industry is the manufacture of cigarettes (London, Bristol, Nottingham, Glasgow, etc.)

9. Disadvantages of localisation. When an area is dependent upon a highly localised industry there is a *risk of structural* *unemployment* (*see* Chapter XXIII) caused by a permanent fall in demand for the products of the industry. This can lead to mass unemployment.

When an industry becomes highly localised towns expand and extend, and with the *growth of conurbations* come over-crowding (with its attendant evils) and traffic congestion.

10. Regional economic planning. For this purpose Great Britain has been divided into the following regions: (i) Northern; (ii) Yorkshire and Humberside; (iii) East Midlands; (iv) East Anglia; (v) South East; (vi) South West; (vii) West Midlands; (viii) North West; (ix) Scotland; (x) Wales.

(a) *Economic Planning Councils.* The members represent experience in each area. They: (i) assist in formulating regional plans, and (ii) advise on their implementation and implications for the regions of national policies. They have no executive powers.

(b) *Economic Planning Boards.* They consist of civil servants representing the main government departments concerned with aspects of regional planning in their respective areas. They: (i) draft plans; (ii) co-ordinate the planning work of the government departments and; (iii) oversee the detailed work on regional studies and plans.

PROGRESS TEST 4

1. What do you understand by an industry? Give examples. (1)
2. Explain (a) the principle of large machines, (b) the principle of the least common multiple, (c) the principle of massed reserves. (2)
3. What is meant by internal economies? Give examples. (2)
4. Why as a firm gets larger does its costs of production per unit of output fall? Is there a limit to these economies of growth? (2)
5. As a firm gets bigger and bigger what kind of returns to scale do we expect? (2)
6. Explain the difference between internal economies and external economies. (2, 7)
7. What do you understand by the optimum size firm? Are all firms of this optimum size and, if not, why? (3)
8. Why, since small firms are high-cost firms, are there so many? (4)
9. What is meant by (a) vertical integration, (b) horizontal integration, (c) lateral integration? (6)
10. Does large-scale production imply standardisation? (8)
11. What factors determine the location of industry? (8)
12. What is meant by private costs and social costs? (8)
13. What disadvantages arise as industry becomes more and more concentrated in certain areas? (9)
14. How is regional economic planning organised? (10)

CHAPTER V

THE ORGANISATION OF INDUSTRY

1. The "one-man" business. This kind of firm has only one owner, who both controls and manages it (he is the entrepreneur).

Such businesses are usually small and therefore usually, but not always, inefficient (*i.e.* economically inefficient, high-cost firms).

One-man businesses are numerically predominant, although their combined output is only a small part of the national product.

Shops and providers of services usually adopt this form of organisation.

Farms in Great Britain are usually small, owned and managed by one man (generally employing members of his family and perhaps, in addition, some outside labour).

Small farmers often do not suffer the disadvantages of small scale because:

(a) *The farmer himself must make many detailed decisions.* When employees number more than a few, management becomes much less effective in agriculture than in industry.

(b) *The advantages of diversification often outweigh the advantages of specialisation* (and large-scale production) because:

   (i) soil fertility is more easily maintained,

  (ii) two different crops in one year are often possible,

 (iii) demand for labour over the year is evened out,

 (iv) risks are spread,

  (v) income is more regular,

 (vi) integration of different stages of production reduces selling and transport costs (*e.g.* farmyard manure makes valuable fertiliser for potatoes; hay and roots are fed to cows).

2. Partnership. A number of people share the ownership of the business. The greater capital available, and specialisation in management, mean greater efficiency than in the one-man business.

Partnership is a useful form of organisation for professional men such as accountants. Each partner is an entrepreneur, that is, part owner; he also exercises joint control.

3. Joint stock companies.

Joint stock companies fall into two categories: *private companies* and *public companies*. Both may issue:

(i) *Ordinary shares.* The holders receive a dividend, that is, a share of the profits after all other claims have been met. The *holders* of such shares are the real risk-bearers. They own the *equity capital* and are the *entrepreneurs*.

(ii) *Preference shares.* These are entitled to a fixed rate of dividend which must be paid in full before the holders of the ordinary shares receive anything.

(iii) *Debentures.* The holders of debentures are *not* members of the company; they are creditors, and are paid interest for their loans irrespective of whether the company is making a loss or a profit. Dividends can only be paid out of profits.

(a) *Private companies* can have as little as two members but must not have more than fifty (not counting past and present employees of the company). Members may not transfer their shares without permission of the company; and no invitation must be made to the general public to subscribe for shares.

One-man businesses and partnerships which want the protection of limited liability become private limited companies. The liability of a member of a limited company is limited to the nominal value of his shares.

(b) *A public limited company* must have at least seven members; there is no maximum. A public limited company has two characteristics which are of great economic significance:

(i) *Limited liability of its members.* This means that a person can become a member of a company without any risk to his personal property beyond the payment of the nominal value of the shares purchased.

(ii) *Free transferability of shares.* This means that a person can sell his shares to any other person should he so desire.

The *effect* of limited liability and transferability of shares is that:

(i) Large numbers of small savings can be canalised into providing *large amounts of capital*, enabling very large industrial organisations to come into being. Hence, a high material standard of living.

(ii) There is a *divorce between control and ownership*: the business is run by directors and managers (who may also own some shares) and the members will seldom have any knowledge of how to run the business they own. People with money but no knowledge co-operate with people who have knowledge but insufficient capital.

The combined output of public limited companies provides a large part of the national product.

4. Co-operatives.

(a) *Producers' co-operatives* are a form of business unit in which the workers are the owners. They have not been very successful in Great Britain; it is difficult to obtain efficient management and to maintain discipline.

(b) *Consumers' co-operatives* are a form of business unit in which the *owners are customers*. There is no conflict of interest. It is an extremely successful movement, possessing a large part of the retail trade in Great Britain (over a quarter of total groceries).

Each co-operative society is a self-governing unit. Each member must purchase a £1 share, although he can invest up to £1,000 (less in some societies), upon which a low rate of interest is paid. He only has one vote.

Profits are distributed among the members in proportion to their purchases. Recently a large number of societies, accounting for over four-fifths of sales, have introduced dividend stamps redeemable for cash, goods or credit to a share account.

The societies vary in size considerably: some have less than a thousand members. The biggest, the London Co-operative Society, has over a million.

The Co-operative Wholesale Society and the Scottish Co-operative Wholesale Society supply the retail societies. The retail societies' voting power is proportional to their purchases from the wholesale societies. The profits of the wholesale societies are distributed among the retail societies in proportion to their purchases.

Although the wholesale societies own a number of factories, the employees in the factories are paid wages; they do not own the factories and the factories are not therefore producers' co-operatives.

(c) *Agricultural co-operatives*. There are two types:

(i) Those which *provide capital* equipment, fertilisers, seeds, etc. A large number of small farmers who own the co-operative can obtain farm requirements in small quantities at the same prices as large-scale farmers; they can use expensive farm equipment which would otherwise be beyond them, their holdings being too small to warrant its purchase for their sole use and which they would be too poor to buy.

(ii) Those which *market the produce*. The farmers send their output to the co-operatives, who grade, pack, and sell. The profits of the co-operatives are distributed to the farmer members in proportion to the amount supplied by each farmer.

In Great Britain many farmers belong to more than one agricultural co-operative.

Marketing boards are somewhat similar to the marketing type of agricultural co-operative.

5. Nationalised industries. They are established by separate Acts of Parliament. They are directed by boards appointed by a Minister of the Crown who is responsible to Parliament.

TABLE 5. THE ORGANISATION OF THE MAIN NATIONALISED INDUSTRIES

Industry	*Organisation*
Coal	The National Coal Board has the monopoly of the production of coal but not its distribution. Of the 259 collieries in operation in 1974, 256 are grouped in twelve areas, each controlled by a director who is responsible to the board. The three other collieries (in Kent) are controlled by a general manager who is also responsible to the board.
Transport	The Transport Act of 1962 set up four boards each of which was responsible to the Minister of Transport who appointed the members. The four boards are:
	(1) The British Railways Board (holds the shares in British Transport Hotels Ltd.—a company responsible for railway catering services)

(2) The London Transport Board
(3) The British Transport Docks Board
(4) The British Waterways Board

Road passenger, haulage and certain other undertakings such as Thomas Cook and Son, and the Tilling Bus group were operated as companies incorporated under the Companies Act with their own boards; they were grouped under a Transport Holding Company, responsible to the Minister of Transport

The 1968 Transport Act made provision for

(a) Capital reconstruction and reorganisation of British Railways,
(b) The setting up of Passenger Transport Authorities to control and co-ordinate local transport arrangements,

and set up three new nationalised bodies.

(1) The National Bus Company
(2) The Scottish Transport Group
(3) The National Freight Corporation

There is also a Freight Integration Council to advise the Minister of Transport and the Secretary of State for Scotland on the provision of integrated freight services by publicly owned bodies. Most of the functions of the Transport Holding Company have been distributed among these new bodies

The Greater London Council is now the statutory transport planning authority for London and has taken over responsibility for central bus and railway services

Electricity Central Electricity Generating Board generates and provides electricity supply to area boards.

Twelve Area Boards are responsible for distribution and sales of electricity.

Co-ordination is effected by the Electricity Council.

The North of Scotland Hydro-Electric Board and the South of Scotland Electricity Board both generate and distribute electricity. In Northern Ireland these functions are carried out by the Northern Ireland Electricity Service.

Gas The British Gas Corporation is responsible for the supply and distribution of gas.

> A National Gas Consumers' Council and
> twelve Regional Gas Consumers' Councils
> protect consumer interests

The form of organisation is that of a *public corporation*. A public corporation has no shareholders; it raises its capital by means of loans.

Each of the nationalised industries is, however, required to pay its way, one year taken with another, and in addition to accumulate reserves for future capital development.

6. Government departments. Many local services are provided by *municipal authorities*. They also build houses and blocks of flats which they let to tenants. Here the ratepayers are the entrepreneurs.

Central Government departments are also producers. In this case the taxpayers are the entrepreneurs.

PROGRESS TEST 5

1. Farms in Great Britain, although small, are usually efficient. Account for this. (1)

2. What kind of firm is likely to be (a) a "one-man" business, (b) a partnership? (1, 2)

3. Who is the entrepreneur in (a) "one-man" business, (b) a limited liability company, (c) a consumers' co-operative, (d) the business of telecommunications? (1, 3, 4, 6)

4. Describe briefly the main forms of business organisation from the point of view of control. (1–6)

5. In what way has the joint stock company been the means of raising the standard of living? (3)

6. What is meant by limited liability? What is its economic effect? (3)

7. What is meant by (a) ordinary shares, (b) preference shares, (c) debentures? (3)

8. Give some account of the co-operative form of organisation. (4)

9. What is a producers' co-operative? (4)

10. Describe the two kinds of agricultural co-operative. (4)

11. How are the nationalised industries organised? (5)

12. Give a short account of the Government, both local and central, in its rôle as producer. (6)

CHAPTER VI

POPULATION

1. The population of England and Wales. The growth of population in England and Wales may be divided into four stages as follows:

(a) *Stage one.* This lasted until about 1750 and was characterised by *high birth rates and high death rates* (between 30 and 40 per thousand). The population increased very slowly and by 1750 had reached 6·5 million.

(b) *Stage two* (1750–1880). This period was characterised by a *high birth rate*, declining slightly, and a *fall in the death rate* to just over 20 per thousand by the beginning of the nineteenth century. The consequence was that during this period of 130 years the population rose by 300% to 26 million.

(c) *Stage three* (1880–1930). This period was characterised by both *falling birth rates* and *falling death rates*. The population reached 40 million by the end of the period.

(d) *Stage four* (1930 onwards). This period is characterised by a *low birth rate* (16 per thousand) and a *low death rate* (11·5 per thousand). The population increases slowly, reaching 49 million by 1974.

The population increased at first very slowly, then very rapidly, then less and less rapidly. It has now reached a stage where *if present tendencies continue*, the population will become stationary or, possibly, decline.

* The *birth rate* is the number of births in a year per thousand of the population. The *death rate* is the number of deaths in a year per thousand of the population.

2. Factors influencing birth and death rates. Some of the factors influencing the *birth rate* are:

(a) *The standard of living.* Where the standard of living is very low there seems to be a tendency for a high birth rate. When the standard of living is higher, it is difficult to generalise.

(b) *Customs and religious beliefs.* In those societies where custom dictates that families shall be large, or religious teaching says that a large family is a good thing, the birth rate will be high.

(c) *Provision for illness and old age.* In those societies where there is no health insurance or old age pensions, a large family is one method of protection against loss of income.

Some of the factors influencing the *death rate* are:

(a) *The standard of living.* Proper nutrition and housing will lower the death rate.

(b) *Public health measures.* These include water purification, sanitation, and vaccination. These accounted for the rapid fall in the death rate in Britain.

(c) *Medical knowledge*, which has greatly increased.

3. The distribution of population.

(a) *Sex distribution.* The population of the U.K. as estimated for June 1973 was 56 million of which $27\frac{1}{4}$ million were males and $28\frac{3}{4}$ million were females.

(b) *Age distribution.* Approximately $\frac{5}{8}$ths of this U.K. population are between the ages of 15–64, just over $\frac{1}{8}$th above 65 and a little less than $\frac{1}{4}$ below the age of 15.

The population is becoming older and the proportion of people above 65 is steadily icreasing.

(c) *Occupational distribution.* The working population of the U.K. is approximately $25\frac{1}{2}$ million.

The *working population* includes:

 (i) employees in employment (excluding private domestic servants),
 (ii) employers and self-employed persons,
(iii) H.M. Forces,
(iv) the registered unemployed.

TABLE 6. DISTRIBUTION OF WORKING POPULATION IN THE U.K., JUNE 1973

	Million
Agriculture, forestry and fishing	0·4
Coalmining and quarrying	0·4
Construction	1·4

Manufacturing (including gas, electricity
    and water)   8·2
Transport and Communications   1·5
Distributive trades   2·7
Professional and financial services   4·3
Miscellaneous services   2·1
Government   1·6
Employers and self-employed   2·0
H.M. Forces   0·4
Unemployed   0·6

                                 25·6

4. The optimum population. The "best" population is a matter of opinion depending upon values which are not necessarily economic. For the economist, however, the criterion will be the standard of living. For him, the optimum population will be that population which gives the highest output per person, *i.e.* the national product divided by the population.

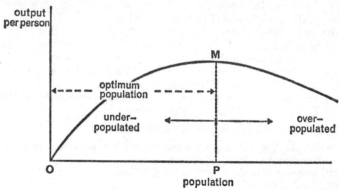

FIG. 4.—*The optimum population.*

In Fig. 4 population is measured along the *x* axis and output per person along the *y* axis. When there are no inhabitants the output is obviously nil. As population increases the average output per person increases; there is greater scope for the division of labour. This is shown on the diagram by the "output per person" curve rising from the origin to point M.

However, after a time a further increase in population would mean that the average output per person would decrease; there would be diminishing returns. On the diagram the optimum population would be OP and the average output per person would be PM. A population greater than OP indicates over-population; less than OP, under-population.

A country whose population is *below the optimum* is said to be *under-populated*. A country whose population is *above the optimum* is *over-populated*.

In actual practice, it is not possible to state the optimum population. In any case, if any country had an optimum population at any given time, this might easily lead to a future population which would not be an optimum. The optimum population will change if new techniques are introduced and new sources of raw materials found.

5. The economic effects of a declining population.

(a) *Production.* If a country has been over-populated a decline in the population will increase output per person: *see* Fig. 4. It is often argued that a smaller population means less specialisation and a fall in output per person, but there will also be more capital per person. The effect on production may or may not be an increase in the standard of living, depending upon whether a country is under- or over-populated.

(b) *Employment.* Changes in demand which cause a falling off of employment in certain industries should ideally be dealt with by a slackening in the recruiting rate. If, however, population is falling the change in demand will be too rapid to allow this, and unemployment will result.

A declining population is an ageing population; the mobility of labour (Chapter XI) decreases and the quality of labour deteriorates. This again aggravates the problem of unemployment.

(c) *Fiscal difficulties.* An ageing population means that the proportion of the working population is falling. A smaller number of people must provide for a larger number of retired people. Perhaps the solution to this problem is to raise the age limit for retirement.

(d) *Urban rents.* The smaller population means a smaller demand for houses. Rents should fall.

(e) *Balance of payments.* A declining population would make it easier for the U.K. to balance its accounts with the rest of the world (Chapter XIX). Fewer imports of food and raw materials would be required and hence fewer exports would be necessary to pay for them.

6. The Malthusian theory of population. Malthus, reasoning from the assumptions that population increased in geometrical progression (1, 2, 4, 8, 16, etc.) but that food increased in arithmetical progression (1, 2, 3, 4, 5, etc.), concluded that population will outgrow the means of subsistence unless checked by vice and misery (wars, famine) or moral restraint (later marriages and refraining from having children).

The theory does not receive any support from events in countries like Britain; the law of diminishing returns to land, upon which the theory can be based, does not take into account improvements in agricultural techniques (fertilisers, new types of grain, mechanisation).

Both population and the standard of living have increased. The means of subsistence increased faster than the population because of the agricultural revolution and the vast quantities of food imported.

Neo-malthusianism holds that the theory is true now of many backward over-populated countries and ultimately for the world as a whole.

PROGRESS TEST 6

1. Give an account of the four stages in the growth of the population of England and Wales. (1)

2. What is meant by the birth rate? What factors determine whether it is high or low? (1, 2)

3. What is meant by the death rate? How can it be lowered? (1, 2)

4. What is the influence of the standard of living upon (a) the birth rate, (b) the death rate? (2)

5. How is the population of Great Britain currently distributed according to occupations? (3)

6. What is meant by the working population? (3)

7. Give some account of (a) the sex distribution, (b) the age distribution of the population of Great Britain. (3)

8. What is meant by the optimum population? Is it a useful concept? (4)

9. How would you define (a) under-population, (b) over-population? (4)

10. What would be the economic effects of a decline in the population of Great Britain? (5)

11. What is the Malthusian theory of population? Does it work out in practice? (6)

12. What is neo-malthusianism? (6)

CHAPTER VII

DEMAND

1. The meaning of demand. *The demand for any commodity or service is the amount that will be bought at any given price per unit of time.*

* It is not possible to talk about the demand for anything without giving or implying the price. It is *always* demand at a certain price.

For each price the demand (*i.e.* the amount bought) will usually be different; normally, the lower the price the greater the demand.

A table giving the demand for a commodity at various prices constitutes a *demand schedule*. Table 7 is an example of a demand schedule. It shows the quantity of strawberries that would be bought in a day at various prices in some imaginary market.

TABLE 7. DEMAND SCHEDULE

Price	Quantity
30p	200 lb
25p	400 lb
20p	600 lb
15p	800 lb
10p	1000 lb
5p	1200 lb

This table means that if the price of strawberries were 30p per lb, then 200 lb would be bought; if the price were 25p per lb, 400 lb would be bought—and so on.

It is important to bear in mind that the demand schedule gives the demand for various prices while all the other factors which determine demand (*see* 2 *below*) remain unchanged.

If the demand schedule be presented in the form of a graph the demand curve will usually slope downwards from left to right as in Fig 5, which shows in graphical form the demand schedule of Table 7.

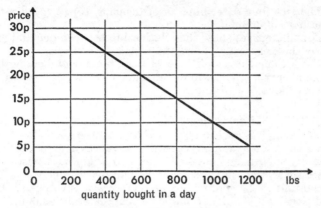

FIG. 5.—*Demand curve.*

2. The determinants of demand. The amount of a commodity bought, that is, the demand for it, will be determined by:

(a) *The price of the commodity.*

(b) *The prices of other commodities.* Buyers consider not only the price of the commodity itself but the prices of other commodities which compete for their limited incomes.

(c) *The income of buyers.*

(d) *The buyers' scales of preference.* Each buyer will prefer certain commodities to others. When he has bought a certain amount of one commodity, say A, he would prefer to buy some other commodity, say B, rather than buy more of A. He could be considered as having a scale of preferences.

His scale of preferences will differ from those of other people because he is a different person with different likes and dislikes. His scale of preferences will not remain constant but will change as time goes on. Advertising is especially aimed at making people put the advertiser's goods at the top of their scales.

The more intensely a person wants anything the higher will it be on that person's scale of preferences. A person's scale of preferences will affect his demand for commodities since it reflects the intensities of his wants.

(e) *The number of buyers.*

The last four determinants of demand, (b) to (e), are the *conditions of demand*.

Demand curves show the relationship between demand and price, the conditions of demand remaining constant.

Each time the conditions change there will be another demand curve. There will be a demand curve for each given set of conditions: *see* 10 *below*.

3. Utility. If any commodity is wanted, that is, if it gives satisfaction, it is said to possess *utility*. As the quantity of any commodity increases, so does the satisfaction to be derived from it; in economic language, the *total utility* increases.

However, the utility (satisfaction) obtained from each additional unit of the commodity becomes progressively less. The additional satisfaction obtained from the additional unit is called the *marginal utility*.

The fact that, normally, as the quantity of any commodity increases, the marginal utility decreases is known as the *law of diminishing marginal utility*.

* Some economists do not like the word "utility" with its connotation of usefulness (Chapter III, 1) and prefer to use the word *significance* instead.

4. The downward-sloping demand curve. The downward-sloping demand curve as shown in Fig. 5 illustrates graphically the general law of demand, which states that *the lower the price, the greater the demand*.

A person will arrange to spend his income in such a way that he obtains the maximum satisfaction from it. The marginal utility derived from each commodity will be equal. This is known as the *Law of Equi- marginal Returns*. If it is not so arranged he will switch some expenditure on the commodity giving less marginal satisfaction to one whose marginal utility is greater. Substitution will take place until marginal utilities are equal (the *principle of substitution*).

If, now, the price of one of the commodities falls, the others remaining unchanged, more of this particular commodity can be obtained for each penny spent on it and hence more utility. An increased quantity can now be bought until the marginal utility is reduced to the same level as that obtained from the other commodities.

As the price of a commodity falls, generally, more will therefore be purchased.

A *change in price* has:

(a) *An income effect.* A fall in the price of a commodity means that the same amount of it can be bought for less money; hence, a part of income is available for further purchases. This may mean an increase in the quantity bought of the commodity whose price has fallen.

(b) *A substitution effect.* A fall in the price of any commodity means that the prices of the *other* commodities are relatively higher, and hence some of the demand for the now relatively dearer commodities may be transferred to the commodity whose price has fallen.

＊ Although more is bought at a lower price this does not necessarily mean that more is spent on a given commodity. The question of the amount spent is another matter: *see* Chapter VIII.

5. Exceptions to the general law of demand. In certain cases —they are not very important—a higher price means a greater demand and a lower price a smaller demand; the demand curve would slope upwards from left to right.

These exceptions are as follows:

(a) *Goods of conspicuous consumption, e.g.* certain articles of jewellery and goods of "snob" value.

(b) *When prices are expected to rise, e.g.* stock exchange securities.

(c) *"Inferior" goods:* an "inferior" good is one that is bought when our income is very low. As income rises, less is bought, *e.g.* margarine.

Suppose the price of an "inferior" good such as margarine falls, then, if the same quantity were bought as before, there would be money available to buy the more desirable substitute, butter; less of the "inferior" good, margarine, would be bought.

6. The total demand curve. The total demand is derived by adding the demands of individuals.

The total demand curve will usually slope downwards, not only because the individual demand curves slope downwards, but also because at lower prices poorer people will register demands which, at higher prices, would not exist.

The demand schedule of Table 7 is a schedule of total demand and the demand curve of Fig. 5 is a total demand curve.

7. Derived demand. There is derived demand for one commodity or service when it is wanted as the result of the demand for another commodity or service, *e.g.* there is a derived demand for flour, which is wanted to satisfy the demand for bread.

8. Joint demand. There is a joint demand when two or more goods are required together at the same time, *e.g.* sand, cement, and gravel for making concrete.

9. Composite demand. Composite demand is the total demand for a commodity which arises when it is required for different purposes and will be the sum of the different demands, *e.g.* coal for households, transport, generating electricity, etc.

10. Increase and decrease in demand; extension and contraction in demand. When more is demanded at a lower price, this is known as an *extension of demand*; when less is demanded at a higher price, this is known as a *contraction of demand*. The different demands at different prices will be shown by different points on the *same demand curve*. The conditions of demand are constant (an example of *ceteris paribus*—other things being equal—so often met with in economics).

✻ Note that these changes in demand are the *result* of a change in price; they cannot therefore *cause* a change in price: *see* Chapter X.

An increase or a decrease in demand occurs because of a change in the conditions of demand (*see* 2 *above*) not because of a change in the price of the commodity; more or less is bought at the same prices.

An *increase or decrease in demand* is shown graphically by a *new demand curve* (Fig. 6).

In Table 8 schedules are given showing an increased demand, perhaps brought about by higher incomes, and a decreased demand, perhaps by a change in taste.

Whereas before the increase in demand 200 lb of strawberries would have been bought if the price were 30p and 400 lb if it were 25p, now, because of the increase in demand. 400 lb will be bought if the price is 30p and 600 lb if it is 25p. On the other hand, when there was a decrease in demand, instead of 200 lb being bought if the price were 30p, only 100 lb would have been bought.

Each schedule refers to a different period when the conditions of demand are different.

TABLE 8. SCHEDULES SHOWING INCREASED AND DECREASED DEMAND

Price per lb	Original demand (as in Table 7)	Increased demand (more bought at same prices)	Decreased demand (less bought at same prices)
30p	200 lb	400 lb	100 lb
25p	400 lb	600 lb	300 lb
20p	600 lb	800 lb	500 lb
15p	800 lb	1000 lb	700 lb
10p	1000 lb	1200 lb	900 lb
5p	1200 lb	1400 lb	1100 lb

These demand schedules are shown graphically in Fig. 6.

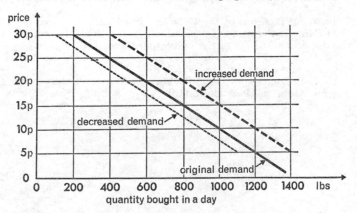

FIG. 6.—*Movements of demand curve caused by changes in conditions.*

* Not all economists use different phrases to distinguish the two types of changes in demand: (1) *the extensions and contractions* of demand, represented graphically by movements along the same demand curve, which are the result of price changes, and (2) *increases and decreases* in demand, represented graphically by different demand curves, which may cause a change in price: Chapter X.

The student should not, however, use the terms "increase" and "decrease" in demand when he means "extension" and "contraction" of demand.

PROGRESS TEST 7

1. What is meant by demand? (1)

2. What factors determine demand? (2)

3. What do you understand by scales of preference? (2)

4. What do you understand by the conditions of demand? What is the effect on the demand curve of a change in these conditions? (2, 10)

5. What is the law of diminishing marginal utility? (3)

6. Why does the demand curve slope downwards? (4)

7. Explain the two effects of a change in price. (4)

8. How is the principle of substitution applied by a consumer in spending his income? (4)

9. What is the general law of demand? Are there any exceptions to it? (4, 5)

10. What is meant by an "inferior" good? (5)

11. How is the demand schedule for a market obtained, given the demand schedules of the individual buyers? (6)

12. Define (a) joint demand (b) composite demand (c) derived demand, and give examples. (7, 8, 9)

13. Distinguish very carefully between an increase in demand and an extension of demand. (10)

CHAPTER VIII

ELASTICITY OF DEMAND

1. The meaning of elasticity of demand. When price falls, demand generally extends; it is useful to know the degree of extension. When price rises, demand generally contracts; again, it is useful to know the degree of contraction.

Elasticity of demand is the degree of responsiveness of demand to price changes.

2. The measurement of elasticity of demand. Elasticity of demand is calculated as follows: divide the proportionate change in demand by the proportionate change in price. If the result is greater than 1, that is, if the demand has changed to a greater extent than the price, the demand is *elastic*; if less than 1, that is, the demand has changed to a lesser extent than the price, the demand is *inelastic*. If the proportionate change in demand is equal to the proportionate change in price, the elasticity is *unity*.

3. Elasticities of demand curves. Three of the demand curves shown in Fig. 7 have constant elasticity. They are:

    (i) the perfectly elastic demand curve (parallel to the *x* axis), whose elasticity is infinity;
    (ii) the perfectly inelastic demand curve (parellel to the *y* axis), whose elasticity is zero;
    (iii) the demand curve whose elasticity is unity.

Usually, the elasticity of demand varies at each price and an example of a demand curve where this is so is the first one. Another example is the demand curve shown in Fig. 5 (*see* Chapter VII).

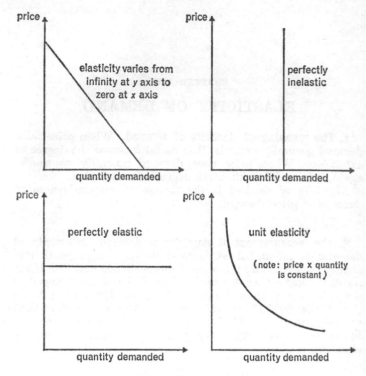

FIG. 7.—*Elasticities of demand curves.*

4. Elasticity and total revenue. In Table 9 the elasticities of demand have been worked out for the demand schedule given in Chapter VII, the demand for strawberries for one day in an imaginary market.

The revenue obtained from their sale for each price (price × quantity demanded at that price) is given in the last column.

It is thus possible to see the relationship between elasticity and revenue.

TABLE 9. ELASTICITY AND TOTAL REVENUE

Demand schedule		Proportionate change in demand (c)	Proportionate change in price (d)	Elasticity (c) ÷ (d) (e)	Total revenue (a) × (b) (f)
Price (a)	Quantity (b)				
30p	200 lb				£60
		$\frac{400-200}{200}=1$	$\frac{30-25}{25}=\frac{1}{5}$	5	
25p	400 lb				£100
		$\frac{600-400}{400}=\frac{1}{2}$	$\frac{25-20}{20}=\frac{1}{4}$	2	
20p	600 lb				£120
		$\frac{800-600}{600}=\frac{1}{3}$	$\frac{20-15}{15}=\frac{1}{3}$	1	
15p	800 lb				£120
		$\frac{1000-800}{800}=\frac{1}{4}$	$\frac{15-10}{10}=\frac{1}{2}$	$\frac{1}{2}$	
10p	1000 lb				£100
		$\frac{1200-1000}{1000}=\frac{1}{5}$	$\frac{10-5}{5}=1$	$\frac{1}{5}$	
5p	1200 lb				£60

✳ The first proportionate change in price is $\frac{1}{5}$ and not $\frac{1}{6}$ as might be thought. The reason is mathematical and outside the scope of this book.

The quantity demanded, column (b), has been plotted against the total revenue, column (f), in Fig. 8.

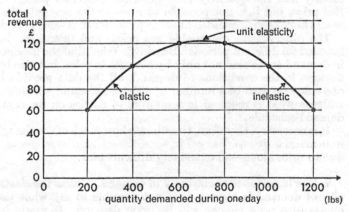

FIG. 8.—*Elasticity and total revenue.*

It can be seen both from Table 9 and from Fig. 8 that *as demand extends as the result of a lower price*:

(i) if revenue increases, demand is elastic,

(ii) if revenue remains constant demand has unit elasticity,

(iii) if revenue decreases, demand is inelastic.

It can also be seen that *as demand contracts as the result of a higher price:*

(i) if revenue increases, demand is inelastic,

(ii) if revenue remains constant, demand has unit elasticity,

(iii) if revenue decreases, demand is elastic.

5. Factors determining the elasticity of demand.

(a) *The nearer the substitutes available*, the more elastic the demand.

(b) *The smaller the proportion of income spent on a commodity*, the more inelastic the demand.

* Do not describe an elastic demand as a demand for luxuries. A luxury with no near substitute has an inelastic demand.

6. Difficulties in the estimation of elasticity of demand. To estimate elasticity of demand it is necessary to compile a demand schedule.

In actual life it is possible to observe the price of a commodity and the quantity demanded for a certain period at *that* price, but it is not possible to observe the amounts that would have been demanded at other prices for that same period.

The observations obtainable are prices and quantities demanded for different periods. Bearing in mind that the changes in demand are caused not only by changes in price, but also by changes in the conditions of demand, all the data provide is one entry on each of a number of different demand schedules, whereas what is required is a number of entries on the same demand schedule.

It is necessary, therefore, to estimate how much of the change in demand is due to changes in conditions to arrive at changes due to price alone—an extremely difficult task.

7. The importance of elasticity of demand. Unless the elasticity of demand is known, it is not possible to say what the effects of a price change will be upon demand. It would be

impossible to predict the effect of any action taken to change prices.

Price fixing by a monopolist. A monopolist (the sole supplier of a particular commodity) may be faced with the problem of whether to raise or lower his price.

If the demand is inelastic at the ruling price, then if he raises his price his revenue will increase (note 4 *above*). It will therefore pay him to go on raising his price until the demand becomes elastic.

Increasing value added tax. The Chancellor of the Exchequer is interested in knowing the effect upon revenue of increasing purchase tax. An increase in purchase tax means an increase in price to the consumer. If the demand is elastic the Chancellor may find that the revenue from this source has fallen. On the other hand, if the demand is inelastic his revenue will increase: *see* Chapter XXI.

PROGRESS TEST 8

1. What is meant by elasticity of demand? (1)
2. How is elasticity of demand measured? (2)
3. Draw a perfectly inelastic demand curve. (3)
4. Draw a demand curve whose elasticity varies from zero to infinity. (3)
5. If both total revenue and price fall, is the demand elastic or inelastic? (4)
6. If both total revenue and price rise, is the demand elastic or inelastic? (4)
7. If total revenue falls and price rises, is the demand elastic or inelastic? (4)
8. If total revenue rises and price falls, is the demand elastic or inelastic? (4)
9. Draw a diagram to show the relationship between total revenue and elasticity. (4)
10. What factors affect the elasticity of demand? (5)
11. Explain why it is difficult to estimate the elasticity of demand in actual practice. (6)
12. Why is the concept of elasticity of demand important? (7)
13. Give examples where the knowledge of the elasticity of demand is of practical importance. (7)

important to realize the effect of each action taken by…

CHAPTER IX

SUPPLY

1. Real costs. The production of any commodity or service means that other goods or services that could have been produced with the resources used were not in fact produced. *The real cost of production of any commodity is the alternative which was forgone.*

The real cost (or the *opportunity cost*) of a ciné camera is the alternative that could have been bought but was not, perhaps a tape recorder.

2. The law of increasing costs. The law of increasing costs states that *for a given scale of production (that is, with given fixed factors of production) sooner or later the marginal cost, then the average variable cost per unit of output, and finally the average total cost per unit of output, will increase.*

This law follows from the law of diminishing marginal productivity: Chapter III, **4**.

In Table 10 are given some imaginary figures to illustrate the law. The first two columns, showing the total output for a given number of units of the variable factor, reproduce the figures which illustrate the law of diminishing marginal productivity in Chapter III, **4**.

In Table 10 fixed costs are constant at £5·88 and variable costs are £4·20 per unit of variable factor employed.

TABLE 10. THE LAW OF INCREASING COSTS

Units of variable factor	Total product	Marginal product	Fixed cost	Variable cost
(a)	(b)	(c)	(d)	(e)
units	units	units	£	£
1	6	6	5·88	4·20
2	18	12	5·88	8·40
3	33	15	5·88	12·60
4	40	7	5·88	16·80
5	45	5	5·88	21·00
6	48	3	5·88	25·20
7	49	1	5·88	29·40

TABLE 10 (*continued*)

Total cost	Average fixed cost	Average variable cost	Average total cost	Marginal cost
(*f*)	(*g*)	(*h*)	(*i*)	(*j*)
£	pence	pence	pence	pence
10·08	98	70	168	70
14·28	32	47	79	35
18·48	18	38	56	28
22·68	14	42	56	60
26·88	13	47	60	84
31·08	12½	52½	65	140
35·28	12	60	72	420

NOTE:

  (i) *Fixed cost* is the cost of the factors of production whose amount does not vary with output. It is also known as "supplementary costs" or "overhead costs."

  (ii) *Variable cost* is the cost of those factors of production whose amount varies with output. It is also known as "prime cost."

  (iii) *Total cost* will be the sum of the fixed and variable costs: column (*d*) + column (*e*).

  (iv) *Average fixed cost* is the fixed cost, column (*d*), divided by the total number of units of output, column (*b*): in the example, £5·88 divided by 6, 18, 33, etc.

  (v) *Average variable cost* is the variable cost divided by the total number of units of output; column (*e*) divided by column (*b*): in the example £4·20 divided by 6; £8·40 divided by 18, etc.

  (vi) *Average total cost* is the total cost, column (*f*), divided by the total number of units of output, column (*b*): in the example, £10·08 divided by 6; £14·28 divided by 18, etc. Alternatively, the average total cost can be defined as the average fixed cost plus average variable cost: column (*g*) + column (*h*).

  (vii) *Marginal cost* is the additional cost of producing one more unit of output. It is the additional variable cost divided by the marginal product: in the example, £4·20 divided by 6, 12, 15, etc.—column (*c*).

The law of increasing costs is shown graphically in Fig. 9. The marginal cost, column (*j*), the average total cost, column (*i*), and the average variable cost, column (*h*) have been plotted against total product, column (*b*).

pence

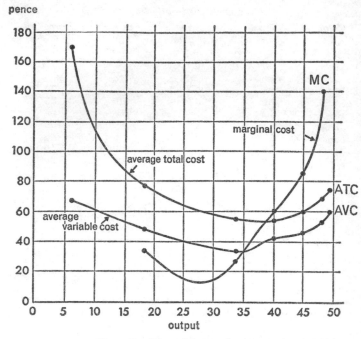

FIG. 9.—*Law of increasing costs.*

NOTE: The point where the ATC curve cuts the MC curve (at the lowest point of the ATC curve) and the point where the AVC curve cuts the MC curve (at the lowest point of the AVC curve) do not coincide with any observations, *i.e.* figures given in the data.

* It is to be noted that the marginal cost curve cuts both the average total cost curve and the average variable cost curve at their lowest points. In other words, the marginal cost equals average variable cost at that output where average variable cost is lowest; it equals average total cost where average total cost is lowest.

3. Average revenue and marginal revenue. In Table 11 the first two columns constitute a demand schedule for a single firm which is the sole supplier of a certain commodity. It means that the firm will sell only 200 units if it charges 30p per unit

but 400 units if it charges 25p and so on. This is shown on
Fig. 10 by means of the line marked "average revenue." It is
the firm's demand curve or, as it is sometimes called, its
"sales" curve.

(a) *Average revenue* is the total revenue obtained from the
    sale of a commodity divided by the quantity sold; in
    other words, it is the price per unit of the commodity.
(b) *Marginal revenue* is the additional revenue obtained by
    selling one more unit.

By selling 400 at 25p instead of 200 at 30p, total revenue
increased from £60 to £100, *i.e.* by £40. The additional
revenue obtained for selling an additional 200 units is £40.
The additional revenue obtained for selling an additional unit,
that is, the marginal revenue, is £40 divided by 200 units,
which equals 20p.

TABLE 11. AVERAGE AND MARGINAL REVENUE

Price (average revenue)	Quantity	Total revenue	Marginal revenue
30p	200	£60	—
25p	400	£100	$\dfrac{100-60}{200} = £0\cdot20$
20p	600	£120	$\dfrac{120-100}{200} = £0\cdot10$
15p	800	£120	—
10p	1000	£100	$\dfrac{100-120}{200} = -£0\cdot10$
5p	1200	£60	$\dfrac{60-100}{200} = -£0\cdot20$

The relationship between average and marginal revenue is
shown in Fig. 10. It can be seen that when average revenue is
falling the marginal revenue will be less than price. It can also
be seen from the table that when the demand is inelastic
(shown by the falling total revenue) the marginal revenue is
negative.

price

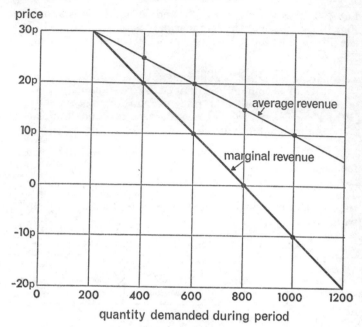

quantity demanded during period

FIG. 10. —*Average and marginal revenue.*

4. Determination of a firm's output. If a firm produces such a small part of the whole supply of a given commodity (because it is one of many firms) that it cannot appreciably influence price by changes in its output, then its marginal revenue is the same as price (or average revenue) and will be constant whatever the firm's output.

If, however, the firm is a *monopolist* (in which case it produces the whole supply) or one of a few firms (an *oligopolist*), then its marginal revenue will be less than the price and both the marginal revenue and the price will fall with increased output (Fig. 10).

The marginal cost will increase with increasing output (Fig. 9).

A firm will produce that output which makes its marginal revenue equal to its marginal cost.

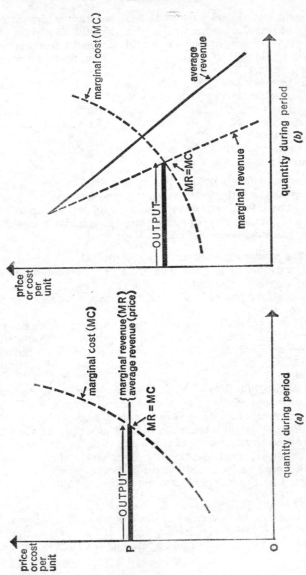

FIG. 11.—*Determination of a firm's output.*

If a firm produced a quantity less than that which equated marginal revenue and marginal cost, it could add to its profit by increasing output since it would add more to its revenue than it would add to the cost of production, marginal revenue being greater than marginal cost.

On the other hand, to produce a quantity greater than that which equated marginal cost and marginal revenue would mean that a firm would be adding more to its costs than to its revenue since marginal revenue at that stage of output is less than marginal cost.

The determination of a firm's output is shown graphically in Fig. 11:

(a) when a firm's output has no appreciable effect on price (when marginal revenue = average revenue);

(b) when a firm's output is a sufficiently large proportion of the total supply to affect price (marginal revenue is less than average revenue).

5. The supply curve of a firm. The total costs of a firm consist of variable costs plus fixed costs. The fixed costs are incurred whatever the output of the firm, even if it is nil. Any revenue above variable cost is, therefore, a contribution to fixed costs.

Only exceptionally will a firm sell at a price which does not cover average variable cost (prime cost) since this would entail making an avoidable loss. A firm might do this during a depression to retain a group of workers who would be difficult to replace.

In the case of a firm which is one of many selling a given commodity or service, the marginal cost curve above the minimum point of average variable cost is its supply curve.

In Fig. 11(a) when the price is *OP* the supply of that firm is indicated by the marginal cost curve at the point where price equals marginal cost. At any other price (provided it is higher than average variable cost—*see* Fig. 9) the supply is similarly indicated by the marginal cost curve.

6. The market supply curve. To find the total supply of a given commodity or service at various prices it is necessary to add the supply of the individual firms. It follows that the total supply curve will be obtained by adding the individual supply curves.

7. The meaning of supply. *Supply is the amount of a commodity or service which is offered for sale at a given price per unit of time.*

* It is not possible to talk about the supply of anything without stating or implying the price. It is *always* supply at a certain price.

For each price the supply will usually be different; normally, the higher the price the greater the supply.

A table giving the supply of a commodity at various prices constitutes a *supply schedule.*

It is important to bear in mind that the supply schedule gives the supply for various prices while all other factors determining supply remain unchanged.

8. The slope of the supply curve. If the supply schedule be presented in the form of a graph, the supply curve will usually slope upwards from left to right (Chapter X, Fig. 12) indicating that the higher is the price, the greater the amount offered for sale. There are *two reasons* for this:

(*a*) Each firm produces (in the short run) a larger quantity at a higher cost per unit (the law of increasing costs).

(*b*) At a higher price, a high-cost firm will produce, whereas at a lower price it would not pay the firm to produce.

9. The effect of period upon supply.
(a) *Very short period.* In the very short run no change in supply is possible irrespective of any changes in demand, *e.g.* the supply of fish landed at a port.

(b) *Short period.* In the short run supply can alter; additional units of the variable factor can be added to the fixed factors, giving rise to increasing supply price.

(c) *Long period.* In the long run the scale of production changes, giving rise to decreasing, constant, or increasing supply price, depending upon the economies or diseconomies of scale (Chapter IV, 2).

10. Determinants of supply.
(a) *Price of commodity.*
(b) *Changes in cost of production.* These arise from taxation, new techniques, new sources of supply of resources, and changes in cost of factors of production.

(c) *Entry of new firms into industry.*

(d) *Changes of prices of other goods* which may mean resources switched to production of other commodities.

(e) *Changes arising from natural causes or political events,* *e.g.* floods, import restrictions.

Changes in supply which are due to changes in the price of a commodity are extensions or contractions in supply; they are shown graphically by movements along the supply curve.

Changes in supply which are the result of changes in conditions of supply, evidenced by changes in the cost of production, are increases or decreases in supply and are shown graphically by different supply curves.

＊ Do not confuse increases and decreases in supply, which may *cause* changes in price (Chapter X, Fig. 13), with contractions and extensions in supply, which are the *result* of changes in price.

11. Joint supply. Often commodities are produced together; changes in the supply of one must of necessity cause changes in the supply of the other, *e.g.* gas and coke; mutton and wool.

An increased demand for one commodity may therefore bring about an increased supply of a joint product and cause the price of this latter to fall.

12. Composite supply. A number of commodities may provide a composite supply to satisfy a demand, *e.g.* tea, coffee, milk, etc., provide a composite supply of beverages.

13. Elasticity of supply. This is the responsiveness of supply to price. It is measured by dividing the proportionate change in supply by the proportionate change in price. If the result is greater than 1, the supply is elastic; if less than 1, the supply is inelastic; and if equal to 1, the elasticity is unity.

A supply curve of unit elasticity is a straight line passing through the origin at any angle to the x axis.

The elasticity of supply depends upon the cost of contracting or expanding the output of existing producers and the costs of firms entering or leaving the market.

PROGRESS TEST 9

1. What are opportunity costs? Give an example. (1)
2. State the law of increasing costs. (2)

3. What is meant by (a) fixed costs (b) variable costs? (2)

4. How are the following calculated: (a) average fixed cost (b) average variable cost (c) average total cost? What is the relationship between them? (2)

5. What is meant by the marginal cost? How is it calculated? (2)

6. At what point does marginal cost equal (a) average total cost (b) average variable cost? (2)

7. What is meant by marginal revenue? (3)

8. If average revenue is falling, what can be said about the relationship between price and marginal revenue? (3)

9. If, with a falling price, demand is inelastic, what can be said about the marginal revenue? (3)

·10. What is a firm's sales curve? (3)

11. What determines a firm's output? (4)

12. Will a firm produce when it only recovers part of its costs? (5)

13. How is the supply curve of an individual firm obtained? (5)

14. How is the market supply curve obtained? (6)

15. What is meant by supply? (7)

16. What is a supply schedule? (7)

17. Why does a supply curve slope upwards from left to right? (8)

18. What is meant by (a) the short period (b) the long period? How does the length of period affect supply and cost of production? (9)

19. What determines supply? (10)

20. Distinguish between an increase in supply and an extension in supply. (10)

21. What is (a) joint supply (b) composite supply? Give examples. (11, 12)

22. What is meant by elasticity of supply? How is it measured? (13)

CHAPTER X

THE DETERMINATION OF PRICE

1. The laws of supply and demand. Chapter VII dealt with the determination of demand, Chapter IX with the determination of supply. It is now necessary to deal with the question of how supply and demand determine price.

Law 1. *Price tends towards that level which equates supply and demand.*

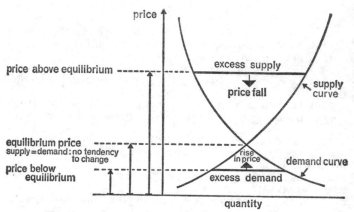

Fig. 12.—*Price determined by supply and demand.*

If prices were at a level which meant an excess supply (more offered for sale than would be bought) stocks would accumulate, and this would lead to a fall in price.

On the other hand, if price were at a level which meant an excess demand (supply insufficient to meet the demand) price would rise.

Only at the price which makes supply and demand equal is there no tendency for the price to change. This is the *equilibrium price*.

Law 2. *An increase in demand (conditions of supply being unchanged) or a decrease in supply (conditions of demand being*

76

*unchanged) will lead to a rise in price; conversely, a decrease in
demand (conditions of supply being unchanged) or an increase in
supply (conditions of demand being unchanged) will lead to a
fall in price.*

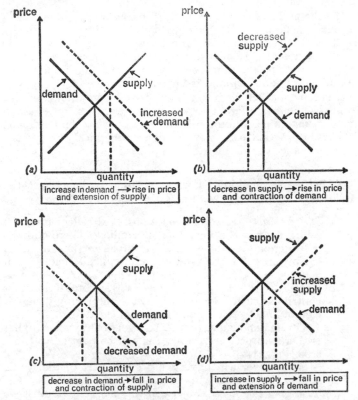

FIG. 13.—*Effect on price of increases and decreases in supply
and demand.*

In the long run conditions of supply and demand change so
that the price changes caused by increases and decreases in
supply and demand are short-run effects: *see* Chapter IX, 9.
This law is illustrated graphically in Fig. 13.

2. The market. The market has been defined by Benham as "any area over which buyers and sellers are in such close touch with one another that the prices obtainable in one part of the market affect the prices paid in other parts."

3. The perfect market. A perfect market exists where there is only one price for the same quality of similar goods, and this will occur where there is competition between many buyers and sellers and perfect communication between them, where the transactions are numerous and frequent, and information about supply and demand is known.

In such a market the buyer is indifferent from whom he buys and the seller indifferent to whom he sells. Hence there can be only one price. Should different prices exist, the buying at the lower price and selling at the higher will quickly lead to the disappearance of the difference in prices.

4. Perfect competition. For competition to be perfect the following three conditions are *all* necessary:

(a) *The product must be homogeneous.* All sellers must be selling exactly the same kind of product. There must be no difference whatsoever, neither real nor imagined. If the buyers think the product is different, it is not homogeneous.

(b) *There must be many buyers and sellers.* Each firm must contribute such a small part of the total supply that it cannot affect price to any appreciable extent.

The demand curve (or sales curve) of any such supplier is therefore perfectly elastic: it will be parallel to the x axis (Fig. 11(a)).

Each buyer will buy such a small part of the whole supply that he too will be unable to affect price.

(c) *There must be freedom of entry into market.* It must be possible for any firm to enter the market and add to the supply, which will have the effect of lowering prices.

In actual life it is practically impossible to find an example of perfect competition. Perhaps the stock exchange (the market for existing stocks and shares: Chapter XVIII, 3) is the nearest.

5. Imperfect competition. If any one of the conditions of perfect competition is not fulfilled, then competition is imperfect. Thus:

(a) Products may be differentiated, giving rise to *monopolistic competition*. Each producer has a monopoly of his own product but competes with other producers making similar products. Since such competitors are not producing homogeneous products they may be charging different prices.

(b) Only a few firms may be competing; their supply therefore affects price. When only a few firms compete, this is known as *oligopoly*.

(c) There may be restrictions on the entry of firms into the market. The restriction of supply leads to monopoly profits: *see* Chapter XIV.

6. The determination of price under perfect competition. Consider Fig. 14. The average revenue curve of the producer under conditions of perfect competition will be horizontal (marginal revenue = average revenue, *see* 4 *above*). The cost curves are as described in Chapter IX, 2. Output is that which equates marginal cost and marginal revenue: Fig. 11(*a*), Chapter IX, 4.

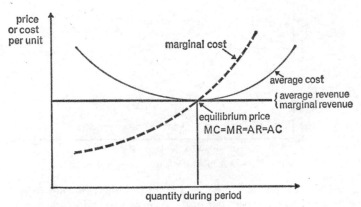

FIG. 14.—*Price under perfect competition.*

Freedom of entry ensures that the price is lowered to a point which coincides with the lowest average cost per unit. It will not be lowered beyond this point, otherwise costs will not be recovered.

It will be seen that *under conditions of perfect competition*

$$\begin{array}{c}\text{AVERAGE REVENUE}\\\text{(PRICE)}\end{array} = \begin{array}{c}\text{MARGINAL}\\\text{REVENUE}\end{array} = \begin{array}{c}\text{MARGINAL}\\\text{COST}\end{array} = \begin{array}{c}\text{AVERAGE}\\\text{COST}\end{array}$$

The firm will have no excess capacity (*see* **7** *below*), and it will be producing its output at lowest average cost.

7. Monopoly price. Monopoly arises when there is only one supplier or a number of suppliers acting as one supplier instead of competing against each other.

Consider Fig. 15. The demand curve will be a sloping one (Chapter IX, 3), and hence the marginal revenue curve falls below it (Fig. 10). The marginal cost curve is rising: Chapter IX, 2. The intersection of the marginal revenue curve and the marginal cost curve will determine the output: Chapter IX, 4; Fig. 11(*b*).

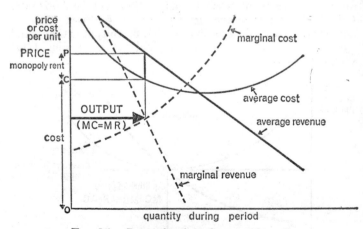

Fig. 15.—*Determination of monopoly price.*

At this output it will be seen from the diagram that price is above the average cost per unit. Average costs include normal profits, for profit is a cost to the firm paid to the owner of the firm, who provided the capital. The monopolist is therefore earning an additional "profit," termed a *monopoly rent*: Chapter XIV.

It will also be observed that he is not producing at the lowest average cost. If he produced more, he would produce at a lower cost per unit. He has *excess capacity*; he is capable of producing more *and* at a lower cost per unit. He does not do so, however, because it would not pay him: Chapter IX, 4.

8. Discriminating monopoly. A monopolist sometimes finds it profitable to split his market up into two or more distinct markets, charging different prices for the same commodity.

This discriminating monopoly is *only possible if the markets can be kept distinct*; otherwise the commodity would be bought in the cheaper market and re-sold in the dearer.

It is *only profitable if the elasticities of demand are different in each market*, the market with the more inelastic demand commanding the higher price.

9. Beneficial monopolies. Not all monopolies are bad, entailing restriction in supply and so raising prices for the benefit of the monopolist. In certain cases monopolies are beneficial to consumers, for example:

(a) *Where monopoly is obviously better than competition* Public utilities (gas, electricity, water, transport) need to be monopolies to avoid duplication of heavy capital expenditure. They are publicly controlled or administered so that they cannot abuse their monopoly position.

(b) *Where the seller requires the whole of the market to make the installation of expensive plant pay.* In these circumstances the price may be lower than that arrived at under conditions of perfect competition. But, again, it is necessary that there should be some kind of control to avoid abuse of the monopoly position.

10. Restrictive practices. Firms often act together as if they were a single firm and instead of competing against each other take part in such restrictive practices as enforcing resale price maintenance, controlling output, and sharing markets.

The Restrictive Trade Practices Act, 1956, requires all agreements made between persons carrying on business within the U.K. in the production or supply of goods to be registered if the agreements contain restrictions in respect of prices, conditions of supply of goods, quantities or description of goods supplied, processes of manufacture, and persons or areas to which goods are to be supplied.

NOTE:

(a) *If neither party is a trade association*, or the goods are for export, such agreements are not required to be registered.

(b) *Collective enforcement* of conditions as to resale price is prohibited, but individual enforcement of conditions as to resale price is permitted. (*See below*.)

(c) *Agreements must be registered* with the Registrar of Restrictive Trading Agreements, who is responsible for bringing the agreements before the Restrictive Practices Court and presenting the case against them.

(d) The Act declares that restrictions in any agreements are *contrary to the public interest* and therefore illegal, unless they satisfy one or more of seven conditions, *e.g.*:

    (i) "The removal of the restriction would deny to the public as purchasers, consumers, or users of any goods ... specific and substantial benefits or advantages enjoyed or likely to be enjoyed by them."

    (ii) The restriction is necessary to protect the public against injury.

    (iii) "The removal of the restriction would be likely to cause a reduction in the volume of earnings of the export business."

If the agreement does not satisfy any of the conditions it is illegal. If, however, it does, the court has to balance the benefits enjoyed against "any detriment to the public or to parties not subject to the agreement ... resulting or likely to result from the operation of the restriction."

As the result of adverse decisions of the Court many agreements have been abandoned or had the restrictive clauses that made them registrable removed.

Resale Prices Act, 1964. Agreements which include restrictive clauses as to minimum *resale* prices are void.

NOTE:

(a) Application may be made for exemptions to be considered by the *Restrictive Practices Court*.

(b) Such exemptions must promote or protect the interests of the consumer or user, *e.g.*:

    (i) where the number of establishments where the goods were sold by retail would be substantially reduced, to the detriment of the user or consumer;

(ii) if the goods would be sold by retail under conditions likely to cause damage to health in consequence of their misuse by consumers or users.

11. The functions of the middleman. Goods do not often pass directly from the producer to the consumer, but through agents, exporters, importers, and wholesalers.

The functions of the wholesaler are:

(a) *Acting as a link between manufacturer and consumer.* This is a form of specialisation, the wholesaler specialising in marketing and the producer in producing.

(b) *Holding stocks until they are wanted.*

(c) *Marketing the products.* The wholesaler interprets demand and may even give instructions to the manufacturer; he often markets the goods under his own brand name. He will blend, mix, and grade commodities.

(d) *Breaking bulk.* The producer sells in large quantities; the wholesaler will break these up into smaller quantities for retailers who want small amounts of a large variety of stocks.

(e) *Reducing the number of transactions and therefore costs.* Suppose there are four manufacturers and four retailers and each retailer wants goods from each of the manufacturers. In the absence of a wholesaler there would be sixteen transactions (4×4). If there is a wholesaler there are only eight transactions, four between the wholesaler and the manufacturers and four between the wholesaler and the retailer ($4 + 4$).

(f) *Financing both the producer and the retailer.* The wholesaler not only finances the holding of stocks but provides prompt payment to the producer while allowing credit to the retailer.

The wholesaler does not exist in certain trades. His functions are then assumed either by the manufacturer or the retailer. Large scale retailing, as in the case of chain stores, and large scale manufacturing where the manufacturer markets his own branded product have in some cases eliminated the wholesaler.

Articles such as expensive jewellery and hand-tailored garments are also sold direct from producer to retailer or consumer.

12. Speculation. The economic function of a *dealer* is the distribution of goods and is part of the productive process.

This usually entails the holding of stocks. The holder of stocks bears the risks of price changes before the goods are sold. In so far as a dealer forecasts changes in prices and acts upon such forecasts, bearing the resulting profit or loss, he acts as a *speculator*.

Suppose the speculator expects a *future rise* in price: he will buy, so that the present demand and hence the price are higher than they would be in the absence of speculation. The higher price leads to an increase in production and economies in use (the demand being transferred to speculators). This in turn leads to a larger supply in the future than would otherwise have been the case and hence prices become lower than would have been the case in the absence of speculation: *see* Fig. 16.

Similar reasoning, but in the reverse direction, applies when a *future fall* in price is expected.

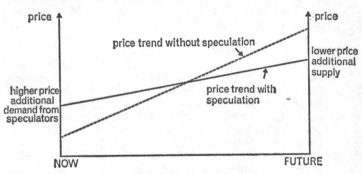

FIG. 16.—*Effect of speculation on price.*

The effect of such legitimate speculation is to make fluctuations in prices less violent and enables producers to avoid risks arising from price changes. It is to be distinguished from gambling on forecasts of prices not based upon informed opinion, which is not likely to smooth out fluctuations.

13. Futures. A "future" is a contract to *deliver in the future at a price fixed now*. There is, however, no intention of actually making a delivery. The contract will be fulfilled by paying or receiving the difference between the contract price and the then current price.

Present price is known as the *spot* price. Future price will not exceed this by more than the cost of storage and insurance (if it did, a certain profit could be made by buying spot and selling future).

Demand to buy future comes from producers who require to know the prices to be paid for their future supplies of raw materials—they thus specialise in their own industry, and do not have to indulge in speculation at the same time. Producers holding stocks will wish to sell future, as a hedge against a fall in price.

14. Hedging. This is a device to protect a producer against price changes:

(a) *A producer holding stocks hedges by selling future.* Should price fall, the loss on stock is counterbalanced by a profit from his future (selling price greater than future spot price). Should price rise, the gain on stock is counterbalanced by loss on the future (future spot price greater than selling price).

(b) *A producer requiring supplies in the future hedges by buying future.* Should price rise, his loss by not buying spot is counterbalanced by gain on the future. Should price fall, the gain by not buying spot is counterbalanced by loss on the future.

15. Advertising costs and price. Advertising is of two kinds:

(a) *Informative.* This is necessary to indicate what products and services are available. Demand is thus directed towards those goods and services which give the greatest satisfaction.

(b) *Competitive.* Its purpose is to persuade consumers that the particular model, brand, or type produced by the advertiser is better than competing products. Often such advertising is necessary for a particular producer to keep his share of the market.

Competitive advertising is wasteful in resources, and by promoting imperfect competition probably makes prices higher than they otherwise would be. But it must be remembered that much competitive advertising is also informative.

Revenue from advertising does enable newspapers and journals to be sold below their cost of production.

PROGRESS TEST 10

1. State the laws of supply and demand. (1)

2. What is the effect of an increase in demand upon supply? (Fig. 12)

3. What is the effect of a decrease in supply upon price? (1)

4. "An increase in demand raises price; the higher price leads to a lowering of demand; it follows therefore that demand fluctuates, first rising then falling." Where is the fallacy in this argument? (Chapter VII, 10 and Fig. 12(a).)

5. What is a market? (2)

6. What are the conditions of a perfect market? (3)

7. What are the conditions of perfect competition? (4)

8. What are: (a) imperfect competition, (b) monopolistic competition, (c) oligopoly? (5)

9. How is price determined under conditions of perfect competition? (6)

10. How are prices determined under conditions of monopoly? (7)

11. What is meant by excess capacity? (7)

12. How does monopoly rent arise? (7)

13. What is a discriminating monopoly? What are the necessary conditions for it to exist? In which market will the highest price be found? (8)

14. When is a monopoly beneficial to the consumers? (9)

15. What are the main provisions of the *Restrictive Trade Practices Act*, 1956? (10)

16. What are the functions of a wholesaler? (11)

17. Can the wholesaler be eliminated? (11)

18. How can speculation level out price fluctuations? (12)

19. What is meant by: (a) futures, (b) hedging? (13, 14)

20. Does the cost of advertising raise prices? (15)

CHAPTER XI

WAGES

1. Wages and earnings.

(a) *Wages* or wage rates are the *price of labour*: a certain sum of money for a certain amount of work, so much an hour, week, or piece.

(b) *Real wages* consist of the actual goods and services which can be purchased with *money wages* which express the amount of money paid.

(c) *Earnings* refer to the total amount earned and are determined not only by the wage rate but also by the amount of work done.

2. Wage movements.

(a) *Earnings and wages may move at different rates* and even in different directions, because:

(i) *Earnings are affected by the amount of work done*, the number of hours worked, or, in the case of piece work, by the number of pieces done. Overtime and short time also affect earnings.

(ii) *Movements may take place between grades.* If there are more higher-paid workers relatively to lower-paid workers than before (as will be the case if workers are upgraded) the total earnings of an industry will increase even though wage rates do not change.

(b) *Real wages and money wages may move at different rates* and even in different directions when the value of money is changing. An increase of ten shillings a week is an increase in money wages. If, however, the increase does not purchase any more goods because prices have risen there is no increase in real wages.

3. Wages and the standard of living. It is real wages that determine the standard of living. There is, however, no direct relationship between wages and the standard of living. Low wages may entail long working hours to obtain sufficient earnings. Earnings which provide a high standard of living for an unmarried woman living with her parents may not be sufficient

to provide an adequate standard of living for a married man who is the sole provider for a large family.

People earning the same incomes may have very different standards of living; not all people spend their incomes wisely.

4. Methods of wage payment.

(a) *Time wages.* A certain sum of money for an hour's or a day's work. This method is used if the work cannot be measured or if it is important that workers should take care and not "rush" the job.

(b) *Piece rates.* A certain sum of money for doing a specific job. This method of payment acts as an incentive to increase output.

The method is not popular with trade unions; it may bring about unequal earnings and cause a rupture in the workers' solidarity. It may produce "speeding-up" and this may lead to rate cutting.

(c) *Premium bonus systems.* Wages are based on a standard time for a given job and a bonus is given for "time saved" (the difference between the standard time and the actual time taken).

(d) *"Sliding scale" wages.* One example is where wages are related to the "cost of living" index (index of retail prices, *see* Chapter XV). Other examples include where wages are related to the price of the product or to output.

(e) *Profit sharing schemes.* In addition to the standard wage, workers receive a share of the profits. In theory the workers' "interest" in the business should increase output, but the share of profits received is often small when compared with the wages. It is doubtful if such schemes have much effect on output and trade unions, generally, are hostile to them.

5. The old theories of wages.

(a) *The subsistence theory.* Wages tend to a level "enabling the labourers to subsist and to perpetuate their race" (Ricardo). Increased wages lead to larger families; the increased supply of labour leads to lower wages (this theory is also known as the "iron law" of wages).

(b) *The wages fund theory.* Wages depend upon the amount of capital advanced as wages and the amount of labour. The wage level will be found by dividing the one by the other.

6. The marginal productivity theory of wages. This states that wages are equal to the discounted value of the marginal product (discounted because wages are paid in advance of the sale of the product).

As each additional man is employed the marginal product becomes less and less: the *law of diminishing marginal productivity*. It will be profitable to continue to employ additional men until the value of the marginal product (discounted) is equal to the wage.

If wages are increased then men will be dismissed to the point where the discounted value of the higher marginal product is equal to the higher wages.

NOTE: The theory can be criticised on the grounds that it is not a complete theory. It explains the relationship between wages and the demand for labour, but wages are determined by both the supply *and* the demand for labour.

The theory indicates that a lowering of wages would increase employment. But a reduction in the amount of spending by wage earners leading to a fall in demand might lead to a fall in investment and hence cause unemployment: Chapter XXII. Lord Keynes therefore criticised the theory as a "static" theory.

7. The demand for labour. This depends upon the demand for the product and hence upon the entrepreneur's expectations of future trade.

The *elasticity of demand for labour* will depend upon:

(*a*) the elasticity of demand for the final product,
(*b*) the proportion labour costs are of the total (the smaller this proportion the more inelastic the demand),
(*c*) the ease with which labour can be replaced by capital (the greater the degree to which it can be replaced, the more elastic the demand).

8. The supply of labour. This depends upon the size of the population, the age distribution, and the laws and customs as to who shall work.

Given the total working population at any time, the amount of labour supplied will depend upon:

(a) *The ability to work.* Increased wages may lead to increased output because an improved standard of living will generally increase efficiency.

(b) *Willingness to work*. A wage increase may lead to a curtailment in the number of hours worked after a certain wage level is reached.

Additional income may not be so desirable as the leisure which has to be exchanged for it.

9. The mobility of labour. This refers to the possibility of changing jobs. It is easy to change from one industry to another provided the worker does the same kind of job, *e.g.* lorry drivers and clerks. Movement from a job in one area to a job in another area is not so easy because of the cost of moving and having to leave friends and familiar places. Most difficult of all is changing the type of job, for new skills have to be learned which may require long periods of training, and often there are trade union restrictions on entry to a new job.

10. Relative wages. In conditions of perfect competition wages would vary according to

(*a*) differences in the productivity of the workers and
(*b*) differences in working conditions, unpleasant work being compensated by a higher wage.

The *net advantages* would be equal for workers of equal efficiency. In actual fact the net advantages are not the same because competition is imperfect. Certain occupations— usually the unpleasant ones—have lower wages than others.

Workers doing different jobs usually do not compete with each other. Each occupation will have its own conditions of supply and demand. These non-competing groups exist because of the immobility of labour: *see* **9** above. People cannot easily change from a low-paid occupation to one which is more highly paid.

11. Women's wages. These are often lower than those of men. The reasons are:

(a) *Their productivity is often less* than that of men (greater rate of absenteeism and labour turnover).
(b) *They crowd into the smaller number of jobs open to them.*
(c) *Employers are often prejudiced*, thinking it only right that a woman should earn less than a man, and some women accept this attitude.

(d) *Women are seldom members of trade unions* and therefore are at a disadvantage in bargaining.

In those cases where a woman does the same job as a man there is a tendency for wages to be the same, *e.g.* bus conductors, civil servants.

12. Collective bargaining. An individual worker is at a considerable disadvantage in bargaining with an employer; lack of funds means he must get a job quickly, he incurs a loss if unemployed and he has an inferior knowledge of the economic situation. Workers have therefore joined together as *trade unions* and have been so effective in establishing a monopoly that the employers have also formed associations.

Many wage rates and conditions of employment are now negotiated between trade unions and employers' associations. This process is known as *collective bargaining*. The advantage to the employer is that he does not have to face wage cuts by his competitors.

Collective bargaining may take the form of:

(a) *Voluntary negotiations* between trade unions and employers' associations.
(b) *Joint Industrial Councils* (or Whitley Councils). These consist of permanent joint bodies of employers and workers, each "to have as its object the consideration of matters affecting the progress and well-being of the trade from the point of view of all those engaged in it so far as is consistent with the general interests of the community."
(c) *Wages councils.* In some industries where trade union organisation was weak or non-existent wages councils were set up. The councils were appointed by the Minister of Labour and are composed of employers' and workers' representatives together with not more than three independent members. They have power to fix minimum remuneration which, if the Minister approves, becomes the subject of a wage regulation order, enforceable at law.

Wages councils have been set up for most branches of the retail distributive trades.

13. The power of trade unions to raise wages. Trade unions can raise wages where:

(a) The increased wages come from increased productivity.

(b) Wages are raised at the cost of employment.

(c) Wages are less than the discounted value of the marginal product (that is, where wage earners are being "exploited").

(d) Where bargaining can obtain a share of the monopoly profits enjoyed by the employer.

(e) Where an increase can be obtained at the expense of the employer, appropriating part of his normal profits. This is only possible for the short period.

(f) Where increased wages can be passed on to the consumer in the form of higher prices. This is inflationary: *see* Chapter XXII.

14. Wage drift. This is the term applied to the *difference* between the *basic wage*, mainly determined by means of national agreements, and *earnings* (see 2 above).

This *wage drift* is accounted for mainly by overtime payments (now very common) and special bonuses, worked out at local level. Since World War II, wage drift has been considerable, earnings in very many cases being much higher than basic wages.

PROGRESS TEST 11

1. Define wages as understood by an economist. Would you include directors' fees? **(1)**

2. How do wages differ from earnings? **(1)**

3. In what ways is it possible for earnings to increase at a greater rate than wages? **(2)**

4. What relationship, if any, is there between wages and the standard of living? **(3)**

5. What are the main methods of wage payment? **(4)**

6. What is the iron law of wages? **(5)**

7. Describe the wages fund theory. **(5)**

8. What is the marginal productivity theory of wages? In what respects can it be criticised? **(6)**

9. Upon what does the demand for labour depend? **(7)**

10. What does the elasticity of demand for labour depend on? **(7)**

11. What factors determine the supply of labour? **(8)**

12. What is meant by the mobility of labour? Do you consider labour very mobile? **(9)**

13. Why do people in different occupations earn different wages? (10)

14. Why are women's wages, generally speaking, less than those of men? (11)

15. Describe the mechanism of collective bargaining. (12)

16. Can trade unions raise wages? (13)

17. What is meant by wage drift and how does it arise? (14)

CHAPTER XII

INTEREST

1. The nature of interest. Interest is the payment made for a loan. For example, if £6 is the payment made for borrowing £100 for one year, the rate of interest is 6% per annum. This is the price of the loan.

This price depends upon the supply and demand for loans. It is payable because capital funds (capital in the form of money) can be used to earn an income.

2. The demand for loans. The demand for loans comes from:

(a) *Producers.* The lower the rate of interest (*i.e.* the price of the loan), the greater the demand, since less profitable uses of capital will pay.

The marginal product of capital falls as more and more capital is employed (the law of diminishing marginal productivity). Additional capital will be used until the value of the marginal product equals the cost of the loan, namely, the interest.

A fall in the rate of interest means that more capital will be used; hence an extension in the demand for loans.

(b) *Consumers.* Loans to consumers for hire purchase and instalment credit amounted to over £1000 million in mid-1964. It would seem that considerable changes in interest rates would be needed to have any effect on the demand for loans by consumers.

3. The supply of loans. The lender receives interest because he gives up the use of his capital and requires compensation for the loss of income he could otherwise earn with it. He will also require some payment for the risk that the loan may not be repaid.

The supply of loans comes from:

(a) *Individuals,* who save for many reasons. If they save as an insurance against a "rainy day" or for the future purchase of some expensive commodity, or because what is saved is what is left over after spending, then the rate of interest is not likely to affect the supply of loans. If, however, saving is undertaken to provide a fixed income at some future date, then the higher the rate of interest the less it will be necessary to save.

(b) *Companies*, in the form of undistributed profits.

(c) *Governments*, who may undertake savings when individuals are unwilling to do so. This can be done by imposing more taxation than is required for the Government's current expenditure.

* Do not confuse an increase in savings, which will lower interest rates (a new supply curve), with an extension of savings, which is the result of a higher interest rate (movement along a supply curve).

4. The loanable funds theory of interest. This states that the rate of interest is that rate which equates the supply of, and the demand for, loans.

This theory ignores the effect of income on the supply of loans; a higher income means more funds available for loans.

5. The Keynesian theory of interest. People may keep their wealth in the form of money, or shares, or real capital, or they may lend it.

If they keep their wealth in the form of money they lose interest: "it costs money to hold money." But if money is lent, interest is earned; interest might be described as *the reward for parting with liquidity*. The extent to which people prefer to keep their assets in cash is called their *liquidity preference*.

The reasons for holding money are:

(a) *The transactions motive*. Money is needed for everyday needs. It is not practicable to pay with share certificates or a piece of land.

(b) *The precautionary motive*. Money is needed as a reserve against unforeseen contingencies.

(c) *The speculative motive*. Money is held in the expectation that prices will fall or interest rates rise.

The demand to hold money will vary with the rate of interest. The higher the rate of interest, the greater the cost of holding money and therefore the smaller the demand to hold money.

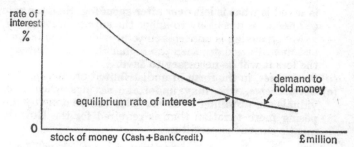

Fig. 17.—*Determination of the rate of interest (Keynesian theory).*

At any time there is a certain stock of money, consisting of cash and bank credit: *see* Chapter XVI. This must be held by someone. *The rate of interest is that rate which equates the demand to hold money and the stock of money: see* Fig. 17.

The theory ignores the effect of income on the demand to hold money; the higher the income, the more money people wish to hold.

6. The analysis of interest. Interest includes:

    (a) *Pure interest:* payment for the use of capital funds.
    (b) *Payment for risk* that the loan might not be repaid.
    (c) *Management charges:* keeping records and collecting payments.

The last two elements, together with the period of the loan (*see* 7 *below*) explain the different interest rates.

7. Long- and short-term rates. A short-term loan is one that is repayable within three months. The short-term rate of interest is generally lower than the long-term rate of interest.

People prefer to make loans which are repayable in a short time. The rate of interest on such short-term debts is the short-term rate.

Borrowers generally want to borrow "long"; they would find it difficult to use money repayable within a short period of time, but since lenders want to lend "short" it will be necessary, in order to persuade them to lend "long," to pay a rate of interest higher than the short-term rate.

PROGRESS TEST 12

1. What is interest? Who receives it and why? **(1, 3)**

2. What is the effect of the interest rate on the demand for loans? **(2)**

3. What is the effect of the interest rate on saving? **(3)**

4. What is the loanable funds theory of interest? **(4)**

5. What criticism can be made of: (a) the loanable funds theory of interest, (b) the Keynesian theory of interest? **(4, 5)**

6. What is meant by liquidity preference? **(5)**

7. "It costs money to hold money." What does this mean? Why, then, do people hold part of their wealth in the form of money? **(5)**

8. How does the demand to hold money vary with the rate of interest? **(5)**

9. What is the Keynesian theory of interest? **(5)**

10. Why at any given time is there more than one rate of interest? **(6)**

11. What is meant by the long- and short-term rates of interest? Account for the difference in the rates. **(7)**

CHAPTER XIII

PROFIT

1. Risk and uncertainty. Risks are of two kinds: (a) those that can be foreseen *and* can be estimated in advance, *e.g.* fire; and (b) those which are unpredictable and whose measurement is impossible. The first type of risk can be insured against, but the second cannot.

The uninsurable risks are known as *uncertainties*.

2. Business risks. Because production is based upon anticipated demand, uncertainty arises from:

    (a) *Changes in market conditions:* changes in the size and age distribution of the population; changes in total income and its distribution; changes in people's wants.

    (b) *Changes in production methods:* new techniques (automation, electronic computers) and discoveries of new materials (plastics, artificial fibres); changes in the amount and ownership of capital.

    (c) *The political situation:* the extent of Government intervention (direction of labour or the location of industry); whether a policy of expansion or disinflation ("credit squeeze") is being pursued (Chapter XXIII); whether there is political unrest or stability.

3. The meaning of profit. Profit is the return made to the entrepreneur for bearing the risk of losing his capital.

Wages, interest, and rent are contractual payments but *profits are a residual payment* and may be negative (that is, the owner would lose some of his capital).

Often a firm earns more than the *normal profits* that other firms in the same industry earn because it enjoys some special advantage over them. Such additional profits, known to accountants as super-profits, are *monopoly profits*—they are of the nature of economic rent: *see* Chapter XIV.

4. Why profits vary. The degree of uncertainty varies from industry to industry, hence "pure" profit varies.

The general level of profits will be influenced by the trade cycle. High profits during "prosperity" periods will be followed by low profits and losses during "depression" periods: *see* Chapter XXIII.

Low rates of interest mean an extension of the demand for loans from producers. This means an increased investment in real capital. Additions to capital are subject to the law of diminishing marginal productivity; increased investment means a lower rate of profit.

The interest rate and the rate of profit move in the same direction, since both are determined by the supply of and the demand for capital.

5. Comparison of the accountant's and the economist's profit. The accountant's profit (revenue *less* expenses) may include any of the following:

    (a) *Management wages:* where the entrepreneur also takes part in the organisation and administration of a firm and his wages for doing this are not included among the expenses, as might be the case in a one-man business.

    (b) *Interest on capital:* where the entrepreneur has lent money to the firm which he runs there may be no interest charged in the accounts.

    (c) *Monopoly profits.* These are profits above the normal profit, the return necessary to keep capital in a particular line of production.

6. Profit as a cost of production. Normal profit, like interest and wages, is a cost of production and is a determinant of price. However, the "rent" element of profits—the part of profits which is in excess of normal profits—although an addition to the cost of production, does not affect price. It results from high prices: *see* Chapter XIV and Fig. 15 in Chapter X.

PROGRESS TEST 13

1. What kinds of risks are uncertainties? (1)
2. How do business risks arise? (2)
3. What is meant by profits? (3)

4. Who receives profits and why? **(3)**

5. What kind of surplus is profit? **(3)**

6. Distinguish between normal profit and monopoly profit. **(3, 5)**

7. Why do rates of profit vary? **(4)**

8. What relationship is there between interest rates and profit? **(4)**

9. What is the difference between profit as understood by the accountant and as understood by the economist? **(5)**

10. Is profit part of the cost of production? **(6)**

CHAPTER XIV

RENT

1. Commercial rent and economic rent. The everyday meaning of the word "rent" is payment for the use of property. It usually refers to land and buildings.

A synonym of rent in this sense is "hire." A television set is hired or rented. This kind of rent is *commercial rent* and must be distinguished from *economic rent*, a payment made to the owner of a factor of production whose supply is not infinitely elastic, that is to say, an increase in the demand for the factor will cause its price to rise.

In most cases commercial rent will include some economic rent.

＊ If an increase in demand for any factor of production causes the price of that factor to rise, there is some element of rent included in the payment for that factor.

2. Pareto's concept of rent. Any payment made for a factor of production above the amount necessary to keep it in its present employment is *economic rent*. It is the *surplus payment in excess of* its *transfer earnings*.

Transfer earnings are the amount the factor could earn in its best-paid alternative employment. The more specific the factor, the less the opportunity of its obtaining alternative employment; the lower will be the payment necessary to keep it in its present employment. The greater part of its earnings will therefore be rent.

3. Rent and elasticity of supply. If the supply of a factor of production is completely fixed then the whole of the return to it is economic rent.

For the supply of a factor to be fixed it must have no alternative uses. A plot of land capable of being used for the production of only one kind of crop and not capable of being used for any other purpose is an example of a factor in fixed supply.

If the supply is not fixed then part only of the return will be rent; the greater the elasticity the smaller the part that will be rent.

4. Rent, cost of production, and price. Rent depends upon the price of the product or service. If an increase in demand causes the price to rise then rent will rise; a decrease in demand causing a fall in price will lead to a fall in rent. *Rent is price-determined.* Nevertheless it is *an addition to the cost of production* paid to the supplier of the factor of production earning the rent, but unlike other costs *rent is not price-determining.*

* High rents are the result *not* the cause of high prices.

5. Forms of economic rent.

(a) *Rent of ability.* This is the term used to describe the "rent" element in wages.

(b) *Monopoly rent.* This is the profit obtained above normal profit: *see* Chapter X, 7.

(c) *Situation rent.* Most payments for the use of land will include an element of rent due to its situation. Sites possessing certain requirements, for example those in shopping centres or at ports, are fixed in supply.

(d) *Quasi-rent.* This is a rent which is earned by the owner of a factor of production which is temporarily fixed in supply.

6. Taxation of rents. Since rents are not price-determining, they can be taxed without affecting either price or production and without causing the factor of production receiving the rent to be withdrawn. This is the argument in favour of a single tax, but it is impossible to determine what part of any return to a factor of production is rent.

7. The Ricardian theory of rent. Ricardo considered that rent was paid to the landowner for the use of the "original and indestructible powers of the soil." Land at the margin of cultivation (which it only just paid to use) received no rent. More fertile land which would give a greater return received a rent over the return from the marginal land.

NOTE: This theory can be criticised in the following respects:

(i) *Land is considered fixed in supply*, whereas most land has alternative uses and the supply of land for a particular use is *not* fixed in supply.

(ii) *Land of greater fertility will naturally receive a higher price.* It is not the same factor of production as the less fertile land.

(iii) *Rent was not considered as part of the cost of production*, and cost of production according to Ricardo determined price. The modern concept agrees with Ricardo that rent is not price-determining, but it is, however, part of the cost of production.

(iv) *The Ricardian theory of rent only applied to land.*

PROGRESS TEST 14

1. What are the two meanings given to the term "rent"? **(1)**
2. What is meant by transfer earnings? **(2)**
3. How does rent arise? **(2, 4)**
4. Can any factor of production earn a rent? **(2, 5)**
5. To what extent is land fixed in supply? **(3, 7)**
6. Do rents give rise to high prices? **(4)**
7. What is quasi-rent? **(5)**
8. Is the rent of a furnished flat in a fashionable part of the town economic rent? If not, is any part of it economic rent and what is the remainder? **(5)**
9. Is rent a part of the cost of production? **(5)**
10. What is the effect of taxing rents? **(6)**
11. What is the Ricardian theory of rent? What are the main criticisms that can be levelled against it? **(7)**

CHAPTER XV

MONEY

1. Barter and money. Barter is the exchange of goods for goods. It entails the necessity of a double coincidence of wants; Y wants what Z has and Z must also want what Y has. This means that exchange becomes difficult and severely limits the advantages of the division of labour.

Money must have been an early invention of man. It replaces the exchange of goods for goods by the exchange of goods and services for money and the exchange of money for other goods and services.

Any medium of exchange which is generally acceptable is money.

2. The functions of money.

(a) *Medium of exchange.* This is its most important function.

(b) *Measure of value.* The value of goods and services are measured in terms of money. It is then known as *price*.

(c) *Store of value.* Wealth can be kept in the form of money.

(d) *Standard of deferred payments.* Contracts can be made in which payment is deferred to some future date, *i.e.* goods or services for money in the future.

(e) *It facilitates unilateral transactions.* Examples of such transactions are the payment of taxes and the making of gifts.

(f) *It is the means whereby the price mechanism acts.*

These functions can be described as "static": they enable a free enterprise economy to work. The following function is "dynamic": it accelerates or retards the economic machine.

(g) *Tool of monetary policy.* By allowing credit to expand, employment may be increased and by restricting credit inflation may be prevented: *see* Chapter XXII.

3. Types of money.

(a) *Coins.* Nowadays, all coins are token money—the metallic content is less valuable than the face value. Prior to

1914 gold coins circulated; the intrinsic value of the coin, the value of the gold as gold, was the same as its face value.

(b) *Paper money.* This consists of notes issued by the Bank of England. They are not convertible into gold. *The advantages of paper money are:*

    (i) cheapness in issuing,
    (ii) convenience in use,
    (iii) ease in guarding against forgery.

(c) *Bank deposits* (Chapter XVI). Amounts placed to the credit of customers' accounts at banks constitute money. A pays B by the transfer of the amount payable from A's account to B's account. The bank owes A that much less and B that much more. The bank's debts to its customers are transferred from one customer to another in settlement of the customers' debts. The bank's liabilities to its customers, known as bank deposits, are therefore money.

    * A cheque is *not* money. A cheque is an *order to pay*. The actual payment is the transfer of the amount from one bank account to another.

4. Legal tender. Any means of payment that people are compelled by law to accept in settlement of a debt is legal tender.

In Great Britain, Bank of England notes are legal tender for any amount, silver coins up to £2 (50p pieces up to £10), and bronze up to 20p.

Money need not be legal tender and in fact bank deposits, which are money, are not legal tender. If legal tender is not generally acceptable then it will cease to be money. In Germany at the end of World War II, marks, which were legal tender, were often not accepted in payment whereas cigarettes often were.

5. History of paper money in the U.K.

(a) *Before 1914.* Bank of England notes of £5 and multiples of £5 were convertible into gold. Sovereigns (£1 coins) and half-sovereigns circulated as gold coins.

(b) *1914–25.* Paper money, consisting of Bank of England notes and £1 and 10s. Treasury notes (issued by the Government 1914–28), was inconvertible.

(c) *1925–31.* Paper money became convertible, but only in exchange for gold bars of 400 oz.

(d) *1931 onwards.* Paper money became inconvertible.

* Nowadays sterling is *convertible,* but *not in the old sense of the term.* A holder of a £1 note cannot receive gold for it (the promise to pay, printed on the note, is meaningless). However, a person living abroad (or his government) can receive gold for sterling. Convertibility nowadays refers to *external* convertibility and *not* internal.

6. The value of money. The value of money, like the value of anything else, is whatever it can be exchanged for. It is, in effect, its purchasing power. A rise in prices means that the value of money has fallen; a fall in prices, that it has risen.

The value of money changes inversely with changes in the price level.

7. The index of retail prices. The purpose of this index is to measure changes in the level of retail prices.

It measures the monthly changes in prices as compared with those on the 15th January 1974.

The basis for weighting the index is provided by the *Family Expenditure Survey,* which covers all types of private household in Great Britain and Northern Ireland. A random sample of households is taken, a new sample each year, and from details of how these households spend their incomes it is possible to obtain the pattern of expenditure, the amount spent on each commodity and its relation to the total amount of expenditure.

The weights are revised annually in January on the basis of information obtained from the *Family Expenditure Survey* for the three years ending the previous June.

Prices are collected each month for a large number of items. The price of each item is expressed as a percentage of the price at the beginning of the year. A weighted average is then calculated of all items and of certain groups of items (shown in Table 12), the weight for each commodity being proportional to the total expenditure on that item. These are price indexes, indicating the level of prices as compared with those at the beginning of the year.

Since the index is computed in the first place with the

beginning of the year as base, it is necessary to multiply the indexes thus found by the indexes at the beginning of the year, which are based on 15th January 1974. This will give index numbers for the month with 15th January 1974 as the base date.

The index of retail prices only measures changes in the prices of certain goods and services bought by an "average" household. It does not measure the changes in the price level of all commodities or services and such an index would, in fact, be meaningless.

Other index numbers do, however, measure changes in the level of wholesale prices of certain groups of commodities, changes in the level of wage rates, import prices, export prices, etc.

TABLE 12. INDEX OF RETAIL PRICES
18th February, 1975

	Weights in 1975	Index (15th January 1974 = 100)
Food	232	121·3
Alcoholic drink	82	119·5
Tobacco	46	124·0
Housing	108	111·1
Fuel and light	53	127·8
Durable household goods	70	119·8
Clothing and footwear	89	121·0
Transport and vehicles	149	132·6
Miscellaneous goods	71	127·9
Services	52	116·7
Meals bought and consumed outside the home	48	120·5
All items	1000	121·9

From Table 12 it can be seen that the price of food increased by 21·3% between 15th January 1974 and 18th February 1975. The prices of all goods and services bought by the average household have increased by 21·9%. The value of money as far as the average household is concerned has fallen.

It is interesting to note that the all items index on 15th January 1974, with 16th January 1962 base date, was 191·8.

8. The quantity equation. This shows the relationship between the amount of money (denoted by M), the average velocity of circulation (denoted by V), the average price (denoted by P), and the number of transactions (denoted by T).

The total cost of goods and services purchased can be calculated by first multiplying the price of each commodity or service by the number of units bought and then adding together the cost of each commodity or service. If this total is then divided by the total number of units bought of all the commodities, the result would be an average price, P. The total cost can be denoted by P multiplied by T, i.e. PT.

The total payments made can be calculated by multiplying each unit of money by the number of times it is used in payment, that is, by its *velocity of circulation*, and then adding these products together. If this total is now divided by the total amount of money, the result will be the average velocity of circulation, V. The total payments can be denoted by M multiplied by V, i.e. MV.

$$\text{Total cost of goods and services purchased} = \text{Total payments}$$

$$PT = MV$$

or

$$P = \frac{MV}{T}$$

or

$$\frac{1}{P} = \frac{T}{MV}$$

This last equation might be interpreted as: "the value of money varies proportionately to the number of transactions, and inversely to the amount of money and the velocity of circulation."

* This equation is not a theory. It is a truism showing the relationship between four variables. A theory of money must explain what *causes* the value of money to change.

9. The quantity theory of money. This states that the value of money is *determined* by the total quantity of money, that changes in the total will *cause* changes in the value of money. The theory is also stated as: "the value of money is determined by the quantity of money, the velocity of circulation and the number of transactions."

The theory provides an explanation over a sufficiently long period. An increase in gold production in 1849–73, and again after 1896, led to an increase in the amount of money. These were also periods of rising prices. Again, gold production fell from 1820–49; this was a period of falling prices.

In a *trade cycle period* (Chapter XXIII), the theory fails to explain changes in the value of money. Rising prices may lead to an expansion of bank credit, *i.e.* to an increase in the amount of money (Chapter XVI). This is the exact reverse of the quantity theory.

An increase in the amount of money may cause an increase in employment and production: Chapter XXII. There may be no effect on the value of money or the price level, since the amount of money and the amount of production (M and T of the equation) may increase in the same proportion.

10. The Cambridge version of the quantity theory. This can be expressed by the equation

$$M = KY, \text{ where}$$

M is the *quantity* of money in existence in a country,

Y is the *total of money incomes* received by the residents in the country,

K is the *proportion of annual income* which residents wish to keep in the form of money.

Regarding K, the reasons for holding money are given in Chapter XII, 5 (the transactions motive etc.) and over a fairly long period is fairly constant. In the short-run K may well fluctuate with the state of confidence in the economy (more money will be wanted in times of crisis).

In the *short-run* if the amount of money is constant and there is a greater demand to hold money, then incomes fall.

In the *long-run* K is fairly constant and change in money incomes will be proportional to changes in quantity of money.

Although the theory helps to explain in both the short-run and the long-run changes in money income it is *not* in itself an adequate theory of money, since money income may change without changes in the quantity of money.

PROGRESS TEST 15

1. What are the disadvantages of barter? (1)
2. What is money? (1)
3. What are the functions of money? (2)
4. What types of money are there in the U.K.? (3)

5. What are the advantages of paper money? (3)

6. What is meant by legal tender? (4)

7. Give a short history of paper money in the U.K. since the beginning of the century. (5)

8. What is meant by a convertible currency? (5)

9. What is meant by the value of money? (6)

10. How are changes in the value of money measured? (7)

11. Describe the index of retail prices. (7)

12. What is meant by the velocity of circulation? (8)

13. What is meant by the quantity equation? (8)

14. What is the quantity theory of money? (9)

15. In what cases is the quantity theory of money a passable explanation of changes in the value of money and in what cases is it inadequate? (9)

16. Describe the Cambridge version of the quantity theory of money and say what it does and does not explain. (10)

17. What is the relation between the level of money incomes and the demand to hold money? (10)

CHAPTER XVI

COMMERCIAL BANKS

1. Bank money. Bank money (or *bank credit*) consists of the credit balances of the accounts of customers of commercial banks. The total amount owing by the bank to its customers is known as *bank deposits*. It is this bank debt which is used as money.

A pays B by ordering his bank to transfer from the amount owing to him by the bank the amount of the payment and to credit B's account with this amount. The bank's debt to A is reduced by the amount of the payment and its debt to B increased by this amount. B has been paid by the transfer of the ownership of a debt, a bank debt.

It may be that A and B have different banks. The effect of this is that the deposits of A's bank will be less by the amount of the payment and the deposits of B's bank will be increased by the same amount. The total deposits of the commercial banks remain unaltered, the total amount of bank money remains unchanged.

✳ Remember that bank deposits are money.

2. Creation of bank credit. A person to whom a bank owes money may require the bank to pay him cash to enable him to make payments to those people who require payment in cash. But most payments are made by the transfer of bank debts. It follows that a bank does not need to have cash equal to the amount of its debts to its customers; that deposits can be many times the amount of cash held by the bank.

Deposits come into being in the following ways:

(a) *When a customer actually deposits cash.* The bank will have so much more cash (notes) and will owe that much more to its customer. The effect on the bank's balance sheet is shown thus:

Commercial bank's balance sheet

Deposits	+	Cash	+

(b) *When a customer is granted a loan.* His current account will be credited, that is, deposits will be increased and a loan account debited, showing that the customer owes this amount to the bank. The effect on the bank's balance sheet is shown thus:

Commercial bank's balance sheet

Deposits	+	Advances to customers	+

(c) *When the bank acquires an investment.* The account of the person from whom the investment was bought is credited, an addition to deposits. The bank will debit an investment account in respect of the asset it has acquired. The effect on the bank's balance sheet is shown thus:

Commercial bank's balance sheet

Deposits	+	Investments	+

In each case the bank obtains an asset equal in value to the bank credit created and in the case of advances to customers and investments the assets obtained are income-earning.

Each individual bank will claim that it does not create credit, that it can lend only money that it possesses and that it can only purchase investments with money, that is, cash.

Let there be two banks, A and B, and let A and B be their respective customers.

Transaction 1. A deposits £100 *cash (say, £5 notes) with* A.

Bank A's balance sheet

	£		£
Deposits	100	Cash	100

Transaction 2. B *borrows £50 cash from bank A.* B now owes Bank A £50 and the bank has £50 less cash.

Bank A's balance sheet

	£		£
Deposits	100	Cash	50
		Advances	50
	——		——
	100		100

Transaction 3. C *pays this money to* B, *who pays it into his bank*, B.

Bank B's balance sheet

	£		£
Deposits	50	Cash	50

After transaction 3 the combined balance sheets of banks A and B are as follows:

Combined balance sheets of banks A and B

	£		£
Deposits	150	Cash	100
		Advances	50
	——		——
	150		150

The banks owe £150 (£100 to A and £50 to B). There is £150 of money; the banks have only £100 cash. Thus, although each bank only lends the money it possesses yet the banking system as a whole has created bank money to a greater extent than its holdings of cash.

In effect it obtains income-earning assets for book entries and these book entries are money.

Each commercial bank will have the Bank of England as its banker and it will consider any balance it possesses with the Bank of England as cash, in exactly the same way as an individual always considers his balance with a commercial bank as cash, knowing that he can always get cash for it (even though he will not usually want to and, indeed, if everyone wanted their balance in cash at the same time, could not). The commercial bank will draw on the Bank of England in exactly the same way as an individual draws on a commercial bank.

Let Bank A buy investments for £100 from B. B pays the cheque he receives from A into his bank, B, which pays it into its account at the Bank of England.

Bank A's balance sheet

	£
Cash and balance at Bank of England	−100
Investments	+100

Deposits are not affected; investments are bought with money.

Bank B's balance sheet

Deposits	£ +100	Cash and balance at Bank of England	£ +100

Combined balance sheets of banks A and B

Deposits	£ +100	Investments	£ +100

Again, credit is created and income-earning assets obtained by book entries.

3. Limitations to the creation of credit.

(a) *The amount of cash held.* Since cash must be paid on demand to any customer requiring it, a bank must have some of its assets in the form of cash. The greater the amount of deposits (liabilities to customers), the greater the amount of cash required to meet this demand. Customers only require, however, a small proportion of their balances to be paid in cash. The minimum cash holding which banks find adequate is between 4% and 5% of deposits.

(b) *The total amount of cash in the country.* The total amount of cash can only be altered by the monetary authorities of the country (the Government and the Bank of England). An increase in the amount of cash means the banks can create further credit.

(c) *The amount of cash the public wishes to hold.* This will depend upon changes in population, employment, and monetary habits (*e.g.* people previously paid in cash and now paid by cheque may now themselves make payment by cheque instead of cash).

(d) *The availability of collateral security.* Usually, before a bank will grant a loan collateral security must be provided.

(e) *Reserve ratio.* Banks are required to hold not less than $12\frac{1}{2}$% of "eligible liabilities" (roughly speaking, deposits) in the form of reserve assets.

Eligible liabilities are:

(a) all deposits in sterling,

(b) funds taken in foreign currencies and switched into sterling,

less

(c) funds lent in the inter-bank market,
(d) sterling certificates of deposit issued by banks (*see* 4).

Reserve assets are:

   (i) Balances at the Bank of England,
  (ii) British Government Treasury Bills,
 (iii) Local Authority Bills,
  (iv) Money at call with the London money market,
   (v) Commercial bills (to a maximum of 2% of eligible liabilities),
  (vi) Gilt-edged securities with a life of up to one year,
 (vii) Tax reserve certificates.

4. The analysis of commercial banks' balance sheets. The commercial banks include the London clearing banks, (Barclays, Lloyds, Midland, National Westminster, Williams and Glyns, Coutts), the three Scottish clearing banks (Bank of Scotland, Clydesdale Bank Ltd., and the Royal Bank of Scotland) and a small number of very much smaller banks.

Table 13 gives a simplified balance sheet of an imaginary commercial bank. It is typical from the point of view of the ratios of the various assets to the deposits.

TABLE 13. BALANCE SHEET OF A COMMERCIAL BANK

	£ million		£ million
Deposits	1000	Coin, banknotes and balance at Bank of England	55
		Money at call	130
Capital and reserves	120	Bills discounted and Treasury Bills	40
		Special Deposits	20
		Certificates of Deposit	5
		Investments	70
		Advances	680
			1000
		Fixed Assets	120
	1120		1120

NOTE:

(i) *Cash and balance with the Bank of England*. About one-quarter of this consists of a balance with the Bank of England.

(ii) *Money at call and at short notice* includes loans to the discount houses (Chapter XVII, 4) repayable on demand and to members of the stock exchange (Chapter XVIII, 3) repayable within one month.

(iii) *Bills discounted and Treasury bills*. By far the greater part of this item consists of Treasury bills (Chapter XVII, 3) which the banks buy from the discount houses when they are nearly mature, that is, due for repayment.

(iv) *Special Deposits*. These are deposits which must be made, when required by the Treasury, by the London clearing banks and the Scottish banks with the Bank of England. It is not possible for the banks to draw cash against these balances. Interest is paid at approximately the same rate as for Treasury bills.

(v) *Investments*. These are gilt-edged securities readily marketable on the stock exchange.

(vi) *Certificates of Deposit*. These are deposits for a fixed term but which can be sold by the depositor. Since they are marketable they attract a lower rate of interest than ordinary deposits of the same term.

(vii) *Advances to customers*. These are either loans for a fixed period or overdrafts. They include advances to firms and to public utilities as well as to individuals. They also include advances for hire-purchase finance.

(viii) *Capital and reserves*. These are the bank's liability to its shareholders—the capital consisting of monies paid by the shareholders and the reserves being the accumulated profits which have not been distributed.

(ix) *Liquidity* v. *profitability*. It will be seen that the more liquid the asset, the less profitable it is; the most liquid asset of all, cash, earns nothing; advances to customers, the least liquid (that is, the most difficult to turn to cash) earn the greatest rate of interest.

5. Functions of commercial banks.

(a) *Acceptance of deposits*. Money can be kept on current account or on deposit account. Money on current account is withdrawable on demand, but earns no interest. Money on deposit account requires notice for withdrawal and earns interest at about 2% below minimum lending rate: *see* Chapter XVII, **5**.

(b) *Granting of loans.* If the loan is for a fixed amount the customer's current account will be credited with the amount. A loan account will be debited. Interest will be paid on the full amount of the loan. Alternatively, a loan is made by allowing the customer to overdraw his account up to a given amount. In this case he pays interest only on the amount overdrawn.

(c) *Making payments for customers.* The greater part of business transactions are settled by means of cheques, orders to bankers to pay. Bankers effect payment by the transfer of amounts from one customer's account to another. This is extremely convenient for the customer and from the banks' point of view widens the scope of credit expansion. A charge is usually made for keeping customers' accounts.

Where regular periodic payments are required to be made it is possible to give the bank a standing banker's order.

(d) *Receiving payments for customers.* Amounts due from debtors can be paid directly into a customer's account (trader's credit scheme), as also can dividends on shares and interest on stocks.

(e) *Issuing bankers' drafts and travellers' cheques.* Where the customer is not known and his cheque would not therefore be acceptable, it is possible for him to obtain from his bank a draft drawn on itself in return for a cheque drawn by the customer in favour of the bank. The banker's draft will be made payable to the person designated by the customer of the bank. The bank's cheque is obviously acceptable.

Travellers' cheques are bought from a bank. They are made out in favour of the customer and are cashable at the places specified.

(f) *Transacting foreign business.* Buying and selling foreign currencies for customers; accepting bills of exchange drawn abroad.

(g) *Providing miscellaneous services of a professional nature.* These include the buying and selling of securities, acting as an executor or trustee, preparing income tax returns, providing safe custody for valuables.

6. The clearing house system. The London Clearing House deals with cheques paid into the branch of one clearing bank and payable at the branch of another clearing bank.

Each day each bank will total the cheques drawn on other

banks and paid into it; summaries will be made, showing totals due to be received from other banks. All summaries will be sent to the Clearing House. These will be checked, and the net amounts owed or receivable by the various banks will be settled by transfers from or to their accounts at the Bank of England.

Only the *net* amount will be transferred; each bank will not only have payments due to it but will also have to make payments for cheques drawn on it.

The work is divided geographically (depending upon the location of the branch of the clearing bank) into (1) Town Clearing and (2) General Clearing.

There are twelve provincial clearing houses dealing with those branches of the clearing banks in particular areas, *e.g.* Leeds, Liverpool.

PROGRESS TEST 16

1. What is meant by bank credit? (1)
2. What are bank deposits? (1)
3. What is bank money? (1)
4. How is bank credit created? (2)
5. What are the limitations to the creation of credit? (3)
6. What are the main assets of a commercial bank? (4)
7. What are special Deposits? (4)
8. Give an account of the work of commercial banks. (5)
9. Describe the clearing house system. (6)
10. What are "eligible liabilities"? (3)
11. List the reserve assets of a commercial bank. (3)
12. What is a certificate of deposit? (4)
13. What is the reserve ratio? (3)

CHAPTER XVII

THE BANK OF ENGLAND

1. The weekly return of the Bank of England. This is a weekly balance sheet, published every Thursday, showing the position at the close of business the previous day.

The return is divided into (*a*) the Issue Department and (*b*) the Banking Department.

TABLE 14. BANK OF ENGLAND WEEKLY RETURN
19th *February*, 1975

Issue Department

	£ million		£ million
Notes issued		Government securities	4,834
In circulation	5,306	Other securities	491
In Banking Department	19		
	5,325		5,325

Banking Department

	£ million		£ million
Capital	15	Government securities	1,215
Public deposits	21	Advances and other accounts	302
Special deposits	935	Premises, equipment and other securities	83
Bankers' deposits	275		
Reserves and other accounts	373	Notes and coin	19
	1,619		1,619

(a) *Issue Department*.

(i) *Notes issued* include those in circulation with the public, those held by the banks, and those held by the Bank itself as a reserve in its Banking Department.

119

(ii) *The fiduciary issue* is that part of the note issue which is not backed by gold. It is now the whole of the note issue, which is backed mainly by Government securities. In the weekly return for 19th February 1975 it can be seen that the fiduciary issue was £5,325 million.

* The gold reserve of the country is held by the Exchange Equalisation Account: *see* 2 *below*. It is not an asset of the Bank and does not therefore appear on the weekly return.

(b) *Liabilities of the Banking Department.*

(i) *Capital.* The capital shown was the amount subscribed by the stockholders of the Bank when it was a joint-stock company. When the Bank was nationalised in 1946 the stockholders were given Government stock in compensation.
(ii) *Public deposits.* These are the Government balances held at the Bank, including those of the Exchequer, the savings banks, and the Commissioners of Public Debt.
(iii) *Bankers' deposits.* These are the balances of the commercial banks, acceptance houses, and discount houses, but not the balances of overseas central banks.
    The commercial banks treat their deposits at the Bank of England as cash.
(iv) *Reserves and other accounts.* These are the balances of private customers of the Bank, including a number of foreign central banks and governments. It also includes the "rest" consisting of accumulated profits.
(v) *Special deposits.* These deposits are described in XVI, 4, (iv).

(c) *Assets of the Banking Department.*

(i) *Government securities.* These include Government stock and Treasury bills bought by the Bank directly. This item changes when the Bank buys and sells securities in the open market: *see* 6 *below*. It also includes Treasury and other bills brought to the Bank for rediscount. This is the item which increases when discount houses are forced "into the Bank," that is, are forced to borrow from the Bank because the commercial banks have called in the loans at call n order to increase their cash balances: *see* 4 *below*.
(ii) *Advances.* These are loans made to its various customers.
(iii) *Premises, equipment and other securities.* This item includes foreign securities.

2. Functions of the Bank of England. The Bank of England as the *central bank* of the country has the following functions:

(a) *To carry out the monetary policy of the country.*

(b) *To issue notes.* The Bank of England has the sole right to issue notes in England. The note issues of the banks of Scotland and Northern Ireland must be fully backed (apart from £4·3 million) by Bank of England notes.

  Notes are inconvertible and the amount of the issue can be readily altered since it is set by the Government.

(c) *To act as the banker of the British Government.*

(d) *To act as the banker of the commercial banks.*

(e) *To act as a lender of last resort.* The Bank of England will always provide money to the discount houses by rediscounting bills or granting them a loan. The discount houses can then repay their loans to the commercial banks: *see 4 below.*

(f) *To manage the National Debt.* The Bank arranges new issues, records transfers, and pays interest in respect of all Government loans. It manages the whole of the National Debt except Post Office savings. The Bank sells Treasury bills on behalf of the Treasury.

(g) *To manage the Exchange Equalisation Account.* The Bank administers this account on behalf of the Treasury. The Exchange Equalisation Account consists of stocks of gold, sterling, and foreign currencies. They are used to support the sterling rate of exchange: Chapter XX, **11**.

(h) *To advise the Government on monetary policy.* The Treasury is, however, ultimately responsible to Parliament for any decisions taken.

3. Treasury bills. Each Friday the Treasury asks for tenders from the public and the discount houses for a stated maximum of bills to be issued during the succeeding week. They will be offered to the highest bidders.

Treasury bills are drawn in units of £5,000 and £10,000 but tenders must be for at least £50,000. Treasury bills are loans to the Government and are repayable in 91 days. For a few weeks towards the end of the year 63-day bills are also issued.

4. Discount houses. Their main business consists of borrowing money at call from the commercial banks and using it to buy Treasury bills, the difference in interest rates constituting their profit.

Should the commercial banks require to increase their holdings of cash they call in the loans from the discount houses, who must then go to the Bank of England for cash. The Bank provides it by rediscounting the Treasury bills on its own terms.

5. Minimum lending rate. The *bank rate* was the rate at which the Bank would rediscount first-class bills of exchange. In 1972 the Bank of England abandoned this discretionary bank rate and replaced it by the Bank's *minimum lending rate*. This is a floating rate and is normally $\frac{1}{2}$% higher than the average rate of discount for Treasury bills established at the most recent tender, rounded to the nearest $\frac{1}{4}$% above.

An increase in the Bank's minimum lending rate means a reduction in advances made by banks because of the higher rates of interest on loans (other rates of interest are related to and move in sympathy with the minimum lending rate). This means a fall in deposits. A fall in the minimum lending rate, on the other hand, means an increase in the amount of bank credit.

It is to be noted that although the minimum lending rate is not discretionary, the Bank of England can by enforcing penal borrowing push up the rate of discount on Treasury bills.

6. Open market operations. These consist in the buying or selling of securities by the Bank of England in the open market.

The effect of the Bank buying securities from the public is shown thus:

Bank of England weekly return

Bankers' deposits	+	Government securities	+

A commercial bank's balance sheet

Deposits	+	Balance with Bank of England	+

In so far as the Bank buys from the general public this will have the effect of increasing the cash balances of the commercial banks, enabling them to create further bank money.

If the Bank sells securities the effect is to reduce bank deposits. The amount of money is, therefore, reduced.

7. Funding. In the case of open market operations, the securities bought and sold are Treasury bills. Only a limited number of these are in the hands of the public. Most are held in the money market: Chapter XVIII. The effects of open-market operations on the amount of bank deposits is, therefore, small.

"Funding" consists in the monetary authorities (the Treasury and the Bank of England) selling long-dated securities Substantial amounts of these Government bonds are held by the public and non-banking institutions. Funding will, therefore, be more likely to reduce commercial bank deposits and hence reduce the amount of bank credit.

PROGRESS TEST 17

1. What is the Bank return? (1)
2. What are the main assets and liabilities of the Issue Department? (1)
3. What are the main assets and liabilities of the Banking Department? (1)
4. What is the fiduciary issue? (1)
5. What are the functions of the Bank of England? (2)
6. What is a Treasury bill? (3)
7. What is the work of the discount houses? (4)
8. What is meant by open-market operations? (6)
9. What is meant by funding? (7)
10. What is meant by the Bank's minimum lending rate? (5)

CHAPTER XVIII

THE CAPITAL MARKET

1. The capital market and the money market. *The capital market* brings together those with savings to invest and those who want to use such savings to increase their productivity.
It consists of:

(a) *Savers and borrowers.* These are persons, companies, nationalised industries, and the Government. Usually the savers and borrowers are different groups but they can be the same, as for example where a company uses its undistributed profits to build new plant.

(b) *Institutions* that bring savers and borrowers together.

The capital market is the market for medium-term loans and long-term loans.

The money market is the market for short-term loans. It consists mainly of the commercial banks, the Bank of England, and the discount houses.

* Sometimes the term "capital market" includes the money market; sometimes the term "money market" refers to the discount market.

2. The new issue market. The institutions which play a part in the issuing of new securities (shares, debentures, bonds) constitute the new issue market. The institutions connected with this market usually also deal with other business.
The main members of the market are:

(a) *Issuing houses.* They arrange for the issue and supervise most of the detailed work. An issuing house may be one of the old merchant banks or one of the new firms specialising in new issues. They often also transact other business, *e.g.* act as investment trust managers.

The reputation of the issuing house is the safeguard of the investing public. Sometimes the issuing house takes up the shares and resells to the public at a profit. This is known as an *offer for sale*.

(b) *Stockbrokers*, who may arrange a small issue, especially in the case of placings (that is, shares sold to selected persons) and issues to existing shareholders.

(c) *Underwriters*, who undertake for a commission to take up shares not bought by the public. Insurance companies underwrite a very large part of all public new issues.

(d) *Investment trusts*. They raise capital by issuing shares and investing the funds in a large number of varied securities, thus spreading the risk and enabling the small investor to increase his security and obtain the advantage of expert management. Many investment trusts underwrite issues which they want to hold permanently and so get them on favourable terms.

(e) *Unit trusts*. They sell units of low denomination to the public, the funds raised being used to buy securities for the trust. A trustee company—usually a bank—will have safe custody of the securities of the trust.

Unit trusts are either flexible or fixed; the flexible trust allows the managers to vary the securities held, usually within certain limits, whereas the fixed trust allows no variation from the list drawn up at the commencement.

Units will always be repurchased by the managers. They are not usually bought and sold on the stock exchange.

(f) *Finance for Industry Ltd*. This company provides capital for re-equipment and development of industry when finance is not readily obtainable elsewhere. It also provides capital, financial advice and computer bureaux for small and medium-sized companies, especially those concerned in technical development.

The authorised capital amounts to £100 million and up to four times its capital and reserves may be borrowed, thus making available some £500 million. The capital is owned by a consortium of bankers.

3. The stock exchange. This is the market for securities which have already been issued. It enables the ownership of such securities to be transferred, thus providing the seller with funds.

The existence of such a market makes it easier to raise capital. The stock exchange can therefore rightly claim to be part of the capital market.

4. The working of the Stock Exchange. Members of the Stock Exchange are either: (*a*) brokers or (*b*) jobbers.

(a) *Brokers* buy and sell securities on behalf of their clients (persons and institutions such as banks and insurance companies) and are paid on commission.

(b) *Jobbers* buy and sell securities on their own account and their profit is the difference between their buying and selling prices (known as the "turn"). Jobbers specialise in a particular market or even in one section of a market.

The stockbroker's client does not come into contact with the jobbers. The broker will approach a jobber and ask the price of the security his client is interested in, without saying whether he wishes to buy or sell. The jobber will quote two prices, the lower one being the price at which he is prepared to buy and the higher one the price at which he is prepared to sell. The broker will approach a number of jobbers until he gets the best terms available.

The buyer will pay (except for some securities for which he must settle immediately) on *settling day*. The period between settling days, known as *the account*, is usually 14 days.

5. Speculation and investment. The purchase of a security for the purpose of earning income is *investment*. When securities are bought and sold for the purpose of obtaining a quick profit, often within an account so that no capital is needed, this is *speculation*.

A *bull* is a speculator who buys hoping for a rise in price (often before settling day) so as to sell at a profit. A *bull market* is one where prices are rising.

A *bear* is a speculator who sells, hoping for a fall in price so that he may buy at a lower price before he has to make delivery. A *bear market* is one where prices are falling.

6. Building societies. Building societies lend money to mortgagors to buy property. They obtain their funds from members of the general public who either invest in shares or make deposits. Most of the funds come from shareholders. Depositors receive a slightly lower rate of interest than shareholders.

Building societies borrow "short" (deposits and shareholdings can be withdrawn at short notice) and lend "long" (they cannot call in their advances to the property buyers). However, although their assets are illiquid they are *self-liquidating*: the loans are being repaid regularly and the societies need not make further advances.

7. Insurance companies. A very large amount of savings, particularly through life assurance, is accumulated by insurance companies. These savings are invested in gilt-edged securities (*i.e.* Government bonds and stocks of nationalised industries), industrial shares and property.

Insurance companies are among the biggest of the institutions which invest savings.

Other institutional investors include trade unions, the Church Commisioners, and educational foundations.

8. Merchant banks. In addition to carrying out most of the functions of commercial banks they also:

(*a*) act as acceptance houses;
(*b*) issue loans abroad;
(*c*) underwrite domestic issues;
(*d*) deal in foreign exchange;
(*e*) deal in stock exchange securities.

9. Finance houses. They provide *hire-purchase finance*. Their funds are obtained from:

(*a*) their own issued capital,
(*b*) borrowing on bank overdrafts or on bills of exchange,
(*c*) deposits from the public (in which case the finance houses are known as industrial bankers).

PROGRESS TEST 18

1. How would you distinguish the capital market from the money market? (1)
2. What part does the capital market play in the economy? (1)
3. What does the new issue market consist of? (2)
4. What are unit trusts? (2)
5. What special financial institution is there for providing medium- and long-term capital for which other existing machinery is considered inadequate? (2)

6. Give some account of the functions of: (a) issuing houses, (b) stockbrokers, (c) underwriters, (d) merchant bankers, in providing new capital. (2, 8)

7. What part does the stock exchange play in the capital market? (3)

8. How does the stock exchange work? (4)

9. What are (a) bulls, (b) bears, (c) the "turn," and (d) the account? (4, 5)

10. Building societies borrow "short" and lend "long," their assets are illiquid but self-liquidating. Explain what this means. (6)

11. In what way do insurance companies provide new capital for industry? (7)

12. What is the function of industrial bankers? (9)

CHAPTER XIX

THE BALANCE OF PAYMENTS

1. The meaning of the balance of payments. The balance of payments is an account of the commercial, financial, and monetary transactions between the people, firms, and government of a country (residents) and the people, firms, and governments abroad (non-residents).

The account will cover a period of time and the balance of the account will show the amount owing to or by a country in respect of the transactions of that period and the way in which it was settled.

TABLE 15. U.K. BALANCE OF PAYMENTS, 1973.
Current Account

	£ million		£ million
Exports	11,435	Imports	13,810
Net invisibles	1,165		
Balance on current account (deficit)	1,210		
	13,810		13,810

Currency flow and official financing

Investment and other capital flows	1,012	Balance from current account	1,210
Balancing item	408	Balance (total currency flow)	210
	1,420		1,420
Balance	210	Additions to official reserves	210

2. The current account. This account deals with the commercial transactions, the buying and selling of goods and services.

129

The goods sold abroad are exports; the goods bought from abroad are imports; the difference between these is the *balance of trade*. From Table 15 it can be seen that this amounts to £2,375 million. Furthermore, it is an *unfavourable balance*. This means that the amount owing to other countries for goods bought is more than the amount owing to the United Kingdom for goods sold.

A country not only buys and sells goods, but it also buys and sells services and these also have to be paid for. The services which a country buys are known as *invisible imports*; the services which a country sells are known as *invisible exports*.

The *invisibles* include payments made in respect of the United Kingdom Government's expenditure abroad (*e.g.* military, diplomatic, and administrative); shipping earnings; personal expenditure by United Kingdom residents inside foreign countries and by foreign residents inside the United Kingdom; interest, profit, and dividends remitted to and from the United Kingdom (*i.e.* earnings on investment abroad); gifts between residents and non-residents.

From Table 15 it can be seen that the invisible exports exceeded the invisible imports by £1,165 million, thus decreasing the unfavoured balance of trade and giving a *deficit on current account* of £1,210 million. This is an *unfavourable balance of payments*.

If the total imports, both visible and invisible, had not exceeded the total exports, both visible and invisible, there would have been a *surplus on current account*, or a *favourable balance of payments*.

* The balance of payments must be distinguished from the balance of trade, which is the difference between visible exports and visible imports only and which ignores other very important transactions which require payment.

3. The currency flow and official financing account. This account deals with

(i) investment and other currency flows, and
(ii) how the total currency flow is settled.

Investment and other capital flows may take the form of

(a) U.K. government loans to, or from overseas governments,

(b) Non-residents investing in the U.K. by making loans to the U.K. or buying shares in U.K. firms or buying government stocks,

(c) Residents of the U.K. investing abroad by making loans abroad or buying shares or other securities,

(d) Credits received on imports or allowed on exports (which are in effect loans).

Investment in or loans to the U.K. means money receivable; investment abroad or loans by the U.K. means money payable.

The result of these capital flows for 1973 was a net amount receivable of £1,012 million. This amount, together with the balancing item, less the deficit balance on current account gave a *total currency flow* of £210 million receivable which was settled by additions to the official reserves.

The *Balancing item* is entered in order to make the account balance. It is the net total of the errors and ommissions in other items.

4. Changes in official reserves. This item consists of changes in

(a) gold and convertible currencies,

(b) SDRs (Special Drawing Rights), (Chapter XX),

(c) U.K. reserve position in the International Monetary Fund.

* The balance of payments usually refers to the balance on current account, but it can also refer to the accounts as a whole.

5. The deficit balance. In the long run, deficit balances of one period must be balanced by the surplus balances of other periods: exports must pay for imports. It is not possible to have a permanent deficit balance, for loans must be repaid, gold and convertible currency reserves are not limitless, and permanent investment in the U.K. by non-residents is not sufficient to balance deficits of serious magnitude.

For the current period a deficit is balanced by:

(a) Loans by foreign governments.

(b) Investment by non-residents.

(c) Sale of overseas investments by residents.

(d) Increasing sterling liabilities.

(e) Decreasing gold and convertible currency reserves.

The short-term solutions to the balance of payments problem are:

(a) *Purchase of foreign currencies from the International Monetary Fund* (Chapter XX) in exchange for sterling.
(b) *Raising Minimum Lending Rate.* Foreign capital is attracted by the high rate of interest, but this "hot" money will be repatriated as soon as this rate is lowered.

In the long run, exports must be increased and/or imports decreased. This may be achieved by:

(a) *Import restrictions:* (i) tariffs; (ii) quotas.
(b) *Deflationary policy:* contracting bank credit leads to lower prices, thus increasing exports and decreasing imports.
(c) *Devaluation of sterling.* This means altering the rate of exchange (Chapter XX) so that the £ does not buy so much foreign currency. This makes imports dearer and exports cheaper. Whether it will improve the balance of payments position depends upon the elasticities of demand for imports and exports.

PROGRESS TEST 19

1. What is meant by the balance of payments? (1)
2. How can a surplus on current account be balanced? (1, 3, 4)
3. What items are found in the current account? (2)
4. What are invisible imports and exports? Give examples. (2)
5. How can a persistent deficit in the balance of payments be cured? (5)
6. What solution is available for a temporary balance of payments difficulty? (5)
7. What items are found in the currency flow and official financing account? (3)
8. What kind of transactions are described as capital flows? (3)
9. What is meant by the total currency flow? (3)
10. What kind of changes take place in the official reserves in settling the total currency flow? (4)
11. What is the balancing item in the balance of payments? (3)

CHAPTER XX

INTERNATIONAL TRADE

1. Special features of international trade. Output is increased with specialisation and exchange. If countries specialise in providing not only those commodities in which they have an absolute advantage but also those products in which they have the greatest comparative advantage or the least comparative disadvantage, their joint output will be greater. This will entail exchange, and all those countries taking part in such trade will be better off (*see* Chapter III, **7**. A table similar to Table 4 could be drawn up to illustrate the gains from specialisation in international trade. Countries A and B replace the men A and B). The same principle will apply to districts within a country.

However, international trade is subject to such economic frictions that it requires special study:

(a) *Great immobility of the factors of production.* Labour is even more immobile between countries than within a country. There are the barriers of language and customs. Often there are government restrictions, labour permits are required and only given in certain cases.

Capital is also less mobile because of greater risks. There are government restrictions on the export of capital and sometimes on imports of capital.

(b) *Different monetary systems.*

(c) *Government restrictions and control:* tariffs, quotas, and exchange control: *see* **3** *below.*

2. Terms of trade. These are the amount of imports that are obtained in return for exports. It is not possible to put this in numerical form since one cannot add together tons of coal, machinery of all kinds, and many other commodities. It is, however, possible to measure *changes* in the terms of trade:

$$\text{Index of terms of trade} = \frac{\text{Price index of exports}}{\text{Price index of imports}}$$

If this fraction decreases, the terms of trade are less favourable— a given quantity of imports will require more exports to pay for them.

If the fraction increases, the terms of trade have become more favourable.

Changes in the terms of trade arise because of changes in the conditions of supply and demand.

> * The *price index of imports* measures the change in the aggregate value of a fixed representative selection of imports as compared with the corresponding value in 1961.
>
> The *price index of exports* measures the change in the aggregate value of a fixed representative selection of exports as compared with the corresponding value in 1961.

There is a *gain* obtained by importing a commodity in exchange for an export instead of producing it.

If the terms of trade deteriorate, this gain will be less. However, the total *gains of trade* are the important thing and these depend not only on the terms of trade but also upon the amount of trade.

It may well be that an improvement in the terms of trade may be accompanied by such a decrease in the amount of trade that the total gains of trade fall.

3. Protection and free trade. Any commodity entering into world trade would tend to have the same price in each country after taking into account transport costs. If there is no restriction on such trade then it is known as *free trade*.

Often, however, a country will restrict imports. This is known as *protection*, which may take the following forms:

(a) *Import duties.* These will raise the price of imports; the home-produced article will meet less competition and so imports will fall.

Import duties produce revenue for the government.

Where import duties are accompanied by a corresponding excise duty on the home-produced commodity then such a tariff is known as a *revenue tariff* and is not a protective measure.

(b) *Import quotas.* Only a certain quantity of goods are allowed to be imported.

Import quotas produce no revenue for the government.

(c) *Subsidies or bounties*. These are given to home producers, enabling them to compete with foreign producers; hence a reduction in imports.

(d) *Exchange control*. Foreign currency is not made available to pay for imports: *see* **11** *below*.

4. Advantages of free trade.
Production will be maximised (law of comparatives costs).

The advantages of large-scale production can be enjoyed because there is a world market; therefore cheaper prices result, and a higher standard of living for people as a whole.

Protection will give the few producers of the goods protected a gain but at the expense of the consumers, whose combined loss is greater.

5. Arguments for protection.
(a) *Non-economic reasons*. Examples of these are:

(i) the protection of certain industries for defence purposes,
(ii) the protection of agriculture in order to have a larger rural population.

The question to be decided is whether the cost in the form of a lower standard of living is worth it.

(b) *Infant industries*. It is maintained that certain industries, if once developed, would be capable of competing in the world market. In the meantime protection is necessary. However, such industries seem to remain "infants" and a tariff once imposed is difficult to remove. Benham suggests that "the best way to give an industry a start may be to subsidise it from general revenue; the taxpayers can then see how much it is costing and can review the position from time to time."

(c) *Improvement in terms of trade*. Part of the duty will be borne by the seller (Chapter XXI, 5); the foreign producer thus receives less for his goods. This means an improvement in the terms of trade. However, the volume of trade will diminish and the total gains from trade will therefore probably fall. If, however, the country imposing the duty has a sufficiently large part of the total trade it may be able to gain at the expense of the exporting country. Such duties may incite retaliation.

(d) *Correction of adverse balance of payments*. Protection is necessary when it is not possible to correct the balance of payments without restricting imports.

(e) *Prevention of competition from exploited foreign workers.*
Exploitation of workers is likely to be increased, not reduced,
if their goods are not bought. Cheaper goods raise the standard
of living of the importing country.

Protection will prevent a particular industry from declining
or help it to expand, but this will be at the expense of the
consuming population as a whole.

(f) *Combating a depression.* Goods spent on home products
will provide incomes and hence provide employment. However, a decrease in imports means fewer exports for other
countries, who therefore suffer loss of incomes. This will cause
unemployment in those countries. They will have less to spend
and this, coupled with retaliatory duties, means they too will
import less and hence there will be fewer exports for the first
country, which will consequently suffer increased unemployment in its exporting industries. The "beggar-my-neighbour"
policy of trying to export unemployment is an extremely short-
sighted one.

6. The General Agreement on Tariffs and Trade (G.A.T.T.).
This agreement, signed by 23 nations at Geneva in 1947 now
has (1973) 81 adherents.

As a result of negotiations (and there are yearly sessions)
many thousands of reductions have been effected in tariffs, and
undertakings given not to raise the existing level of duties.
However, quantitative restrictions on imports are widespread.

7. The European Economic Community (E.E.C.). It originally
consisted of six countries: Belgium, France, the Federal
German Republic, Italy, Luxembourg, and the Netherlands.
Since the 1st January 1968 all industrial tariff barriers between
the six have been removed. They also apply a common external
tariff.

In 1973 the E.E.C. was enlarged by the addition of three new
members; the United Kingdom, Ireland and Denmark.

The United Kingdom is to lower her tariffs within the community in five stages over some $4\frac{1}{2}$ years and at the same time
progressively raise her tariffs to countries outside the community.

8. The European Free Trade Association (E.F.T.A.). The
E.F.T.A. countries are Sweden, Norway, Austria, Portugal,
Switzerland, Finland and Iceland.

Protective tariffs and quotas on trade in industrial products between members of E.F.T.A. were eliminated finally in December 1967. There is no common external tariff.

9. The gold standard. The full gold standard means that any banknote can be exchanged for gold. The amount of cash in the country therefore depends upon the stock of gold. If the stock of gold increases, the quantity of cash and money expands. If the stock decreases, the amount of money decreases.

The advantage of the gold standard is that no balance of payments problem arises. The deficit or surplus is corrected automatically:

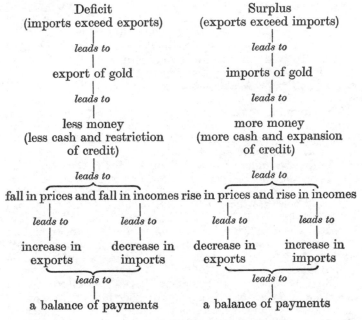

Deficit
(imports exceed exports)

leads to

export of gold

leads to

less money
(less cash and restriction
of credit)

leads to

fall in prices and fall in incomes

leads to   *leads to*

increase in   decrease in
exports   imports

leads to

a balance of payments

Surplus
(exports exceed imports)

leads to

imports of gold

leads to

more money
(more cash and expansion
of credit)

leads to

rise in prices and rise in incomes

leads to   *leads to*

decrease in   increase in
exports   imports

leads to

a balance of payments

The disadvantage of the gold standard is that changes in the stocks of gold cause fluctuations in production and employment.

An expanding economy requires an increasing amount of money, but the amount of money under the gold standard depends upon the stock of gold in the country.

Changes in the stocks of gold cause changes in the amount of money, which cause changes in prices; hence changes in demand and consequent changes in production and employment.

10. Foreign exchange rates. These are the prices of foreign currencies. As an example, the rate of exchange for French francs is at the time of writing 10 to the £: this is the price of £1 for a person possessing French francs and wishing to buy £1 sterling. Alternatively, it means that the price of a French franc is 10p.

Like all prices, exchange rates are determined by supply and demand. The demand for foreign exchange comes from importers and the supply from exporters. To the demand and supply from trade must be added the supply and demand arising from capital transactions (Chapter XIX).

If no action is taken to control the rates of exchange and they are allowed to move freely in accordance with the supply of and demand for foreign currency they are known as *free exchange rates* or *flexible exchange rates*, or *floating exchange rates*.

The advantage of free exchange rates is that a country can pursue any monetary policy necessary to maintain full employment or prevent inflation without incurring a balance of payments problem (Chapter XXII).

The disadvantage of free exchange rates is that they will fluctuate, and this is harmful to international trade.

Euro-dollars are deposits of U.S. dollars with commercial banks outside the United States, and the Euro-dollar market is made up of banks situated mainly in London and other European centres (including the overseas branches of U.S. banks) which bid for the U.S. dollar deposits and offer loans in U.S. dollars.

A market arises in Euro-dollars in the following way. A depositor of dollars can earn a competitive interest rate on his Euro-dollar account, whereas in the United States the Federal Reserve forbids interest on demand deposits (known as current accounts in this country) and restricts interest on time deposits (known as deposit accounts in this country). The European bank's motive for dealing in Euro-dollars is that it can re-lend the deposited dollar at a higher rate of interest than it pays.

Similarly with other *Euro-currencies*, such as sterling, marks, Swiss francs, lire and guilders. These are deposits of such currencies in banks outside the countries where each of these currencies circulates.

11. Exchange control. This means that it is not possible to purchase foreign currency freely. Application must be made to the central bank, which will sell only limited amounts and for approved purposes. Exporters cannot retain any foreign currencies acquired as these must also be sold to the central bank.

Since the end of 1958 sterling earned by non-residents has been freely convertible.

Great Britain has an Exchange Equalisation Account (Chapter XVII, 2) and by means of selling or purchasing any foreign currency in return for sterling or gold it can maintain the par value of sterling within narrow limits.

The *par value* is the amount of gold for which a unit of currency is exchangeable. There are fixed exchange rates (varying within narrow limits) between those countries whose currencies have par values.

The currencies of all members of the International Monetary Fund have par values: *see* **12** *below.*

12. The International Monetary Fund (I.M.F.). The I.M.F. (agreement drafted at Bretton Woods, 1944) now has 125 members (1972). The objects of the fund are:

(i) to promote international monetary co-operation,
(ii) to provide financial aid to members having balance of payment difficulties,
(iii) to provide for the growth of international liquidity by means of Special Drawing Rights.

Short-term financial aid is provided to those member countries who have balance of payments difficulties. The usual way of doing this is to provide the foreign currencies they require in exchange for their own.

The Fund's resources are supplied by the members. Each has a *quota* determined by its amount of international trade. Each member pays into the Fund 25% of this quota in gold and the remainder in its own currency (the total pool amounts to the equivalent of $30,000 million).

The drawing rights of members are limited so that the Fund's holdings of its currency must not rise by more than 25% of its quota in any twelve-month period, nor exceed 200% of its quota. Members are expected to repay within three to five years, but if a country's reserves are increasing rapidly it is expected to repay more quickly.

Additionally, members have *Special Drawing Rights*. The I.M.F. keeps transactions in these special Drawing Rights in a separate Special Drawing Account.

Special Drawing Rights (SDRs). SDRs are in effect a reserve asset created by the International Monetary Fund. They serve the same purpose as gold reserves and for this reason are called "paper gold."

The amount to be created each year is decided by the members of the I.M.F. but the allocation among the member countries is in proportion to their quotas.

The value of 1 SDR is equal in value to $\frac{1}{35}$ oz. of gold. All participating countries agree to accept SDRs in settlement of international indebtedness at this fixed value.

13. The International Bank for Reconstruction and Development (the World Bank). This was also set up at the Bretton Woods Conference. It has more or less the same membership as the I.M.F.

(a) *The objects* are:

(i) *To help reconstruct productive capacity destroyed during the war.*

(ii) *To help develop economic resources and the growth of productive power*, particularly in backward and under-developed countries.

(b) *The methods* of achieving these objects are:

(i) Each member is liable for a quota.

(ii) In addition the Banks issues bonds.

(iii) The Bank normally lends only against specific projects and confines its participation to financing the foreign exchange part. It charges interest on the loans granted.

PROGRESS TEST 20

1. State the law of comparative advantage (Chapter III, **7**)

2. How does international trade differ from trade within a country? **(1)**

3. What are the advantages of international trade? **(1)**

4. What is meant by the "terms of trade"? (2)

5. What are the gains of trade? (2)

6. How can changes in the terms of trade be measured? (2)

7. What forms can protection take? (3)

8. What are the advantages of free trade? (4)

9. What arguments are there in favour of protection? (5)

10. What is the G.A.T.T.? (6)

11. What is the E.E.C.? (7)

12. What is the E.F.T.A.? (8)

13. How did the gold standard work? (9)

14. What are the advantages and disadvantages of the gold standard? (9)

15. How does a system of free exchange rates work? (10)

16. What are Euro-dollars? (10)

17. Give some account of the Euro-dollar market. (10)

18. How does exchange control work? (11)

19. What are the functions of the I.M.F.? (12)

20. What are SDRs? (12)

21. What is the World Bank? How does it work? (13)

CHAPTER XXI

PUBLIC FINANCE

1. Government expenditure and revenue. A government has very heavy expenditure, and to meet this raises money by taxation.

(a) *Expenditure:*

   (i) *Supply services:* armed forces and defence.
  (ii) *Consolidated fund services:* interest on the National Debt and its cost of management.
 (iii) *Civil and revenue departments:* social services (health, education, social security payments); agricultural and food subsidies; assistance to local authorities (police, roads, housing); general services (tax collection, law and order).

(b) *Revenue:*

   (i) *Taxes on income and capital:* income tax, corporation tax capital transfer tax.
  (ii) *Expenditure taxes* (also described as indirect taxes): value added tax, betting tax, entertainments tax, import duties, stamp duties, excise duties.
 (iii) *Non-tax revenue:* dividends from shares owned by the Government (*e.g.* British Petroleum Co. Ltd.), interest on loans, income from trading.

2. Definition of tax. A tax is a compulsory contribution made by the taxpayer to the State towards its expenditure. It is not a price, for the tax payable bears no relation to the services received.

3. The aims of taxation. Although the main purpose of taxation is to *raise revenue to meet expenditure*, it can serve other very important ends. It can be used:

(a) *To lessen the inequality of incomes.* This is achieved by progressive taxation—the higher the income the higher the *rate* of tax. Death duties, which are also progressive, help to disperse large fortunes, which in turn means the reduction of large incomes.

Social security payments provide necessary incomes to unemployed, sick, and retired people.

(b) *As an instrument of control of the level of economic activity.* Deficit budgeting (raising insufficient revenue from taxation to cover expenditure) is the fiscal policy adopted to combat general unemployment: Chapter XXII.

Surplus budgeting (more revenue collected than is necessary) is a measure to combat inflation: *see* Chapter XXII.

(c) *To influence production and consumption.* By imposing purchase taxes and import duties the pattern of production and consumption can be changed.

4. The canons of taxation. These are the rules to be applied in devising a system of taxation:

(a) *Ability of the taxpayer to pay.* This implies progressive taxation (*see* 3 *above*) and allowances for dependants.

(b) *Convenience.* Payment should be convenient for the taxpayer (P.A.Y.E. observes this rule).

(c) *Certainty.* There must be no doubt as to the amount payable.

(d) *Economy.* A tax should not be expensive to collect.

(e) *Effectiveness.* The tax should yield sufficient revenue to the government or, if the purpose of the tax is in persuance of some other aim (*e.g.* discouraging the consumption of certain goods), it should be capable of achieving that aim.

(f) *Minimal effect on output.* A tax should not affect willingness to work nor discourage investment.

(g) *Flexibility.* A tax should be capable of being easily altered to meet changing fiscal requirements (purchase tax observes this rule).

Canons (a) to (d) were first stated by Adam Smith, although his interpretation of ability to pay differed from that given above.

5. The incidence of expenditure taxes. Although the impact of such a tax is on the seller—that is to say, he pays it—all, part, or none (depending upon the respective elasticities of supply and demand) is shifted on to—that is, borne by—the consumer.

This is shown in Fig. 18. In Chapter IX it was demonstrated that the supply curve was a cost curve. If an expenditure tax is imposed this will raise the cost by the amount of the tax. It will be seen, however, that the new price is not increased by the same amount as the tax; but the producer has succeeded in passing on some of the tax.

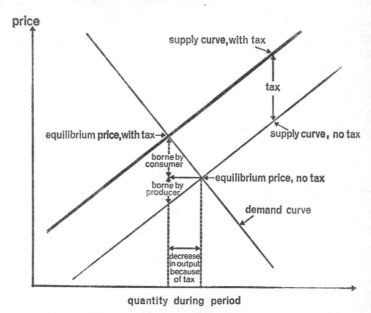

FIG. 18.—*Incidence of expenditure taxes.*

The more inelastic the *supply*, the smaller is the amount of tax shifted on to the consumer and the smaller the decrease in output: consequently the greater the yield of revenue.

The more inelastic the *demand*, the greater is the amount shifted on to the consumer, but the smaller the decrease in output: consequently the greater the yield of revenue.

In the long-run supply becomes more elastic and the burden falling on the consumer becomes greater.

6. Advantages and disadvantages of expenditure taxes.

(a) *The advantages* of expenditure taxes are that:

(i) *They are easy to collect.* It would not be possible to raise all the revenue required by income tax since the rate would be prohibitive. Expenditure taxes yield revenue immediately they are imposed.

(ii) *They act as a regulator of the economy.* Levying taxes on goods will cause demand to fall—a measure against rising prices. It may divert goods to the export market. Import duties may be levied to reduce imports in order to correct an adverse balance of payments or to "protect" some industry.

(b) *The disadvantages* of expenditure taxes are that:

(i) *They are regressive.* The amount paid by a poor man will be a relatively larger part of his income than that of a rich man.

(ii) *They are discriminating* The person who buys goods upon which taxes are levied, *e.g.* alcoholic drinks, tobacco, petrol, pays taxes while the non-drinking, non-smoking, non-motorist escapes.

(iii) *They may cause demands for wage increases.* If a tax is imposed on goods entering into everyday household expenditure, the index of retail prices will rise. A rise in this index gives support to wage-increase demands.

7. Economic effects of taxation.

(a) *Disincentive to work.* In effect taxation on income from work is a reduction in wage rates. The result will be an increase in the amount of work or a decrease, depending upon the elasticity of demand for income.

Because the marginal rate of income tax is steeply progressive absenteeism is encouraged and overtime discouraged, with consequent loss of production.

Expenditure taxes may, however, intensify the incentive to work, more income being required to obtain the same amount of goods.

In point of fact, both expenditure taxes and income taxes have steadily increased over the years since the end of World War II, yet the amount of overtime has also steadily increased.

(b) *Disincentive to saving.* Since taxation leaves less available for saving, people will generally save less, but it does depend upon the purpose of saving and it is possible that some people will work harder in order to save as much as before.

Much saving used to be for provision against illness, unemployment, and old age. This is now covered by social insurance.

A great part of saving is now provided by institutions (*e.g.* insurance companies), the Government and public companies (in the form of undistributed profits).

(c) *Disincentive to investment.* Entrepreneurs will not undertake new ventures if taxation is going to take away too large a part of their profits.

(d) *Diversion of production* from higher-taxed industries to lower-taxed industries.

(e) *Potentially inflationary.* Where tax is shifted on to the consumer, higher prices may give rise to demands for higher wages, leading to higher costs, leading to higher prices of other commodities.

8. The National Debt. The National Debt consists of the amounts borrowed by the Government to meet expenditure when its revenue from taxation and trading has been insufficient. It is mainly owed to residents of Great Britain and is therefore mainly *internal debt.* It consists of:

(a) *Short-term debt:* mainly Treasury bills and loans repayable at short notice or on demand, such as National Savings certificates and Post Office savings.
(b) *Medium-term debts* repayable between one and ten years from the date of issue. These are mainly bonds.
(c) *Long-term debt* repayable more than ten years after issue, *e.g.* 4% Funding Loan 1960–90 (the Government will repay sometime between 1960 and 1990).

The National Debt can be:

(a) *Unfunded debt:* loans to be repaid;
(b) *Funded debt:* loans which the Government is not required to repay.

9. Local government finance. Much of the work of government is carried out by local authorities, *e.g.* the provision of education, police, and health services.

Local authorities obtain their revenue from: (*a*) central Government grants; (*b*) rates; (*c*) trading, rents, and interest.

Rates are taxes levied by local authorities on the value of land and buildings occupied.

(a) *Advantages of rates as a form of taxation:*

(i) *Stable yield* not varying with the state of trade.

(ii) *Easy to collect* since the occupier is responsible for actual payment.

(iii) *They are a method of taxation not used by central Government.*

(b) *Disadvantages of rates as a form of taxation:*

(i) *May be regressive.* The building occupied may bear no relation to ability to pay.

(ii) *Inflexible.* They cannot easily be changed to meet desirable expenditure.

(iii) *Inequitable* between districts.

PROGRESS TEST 21

1. What kinds of taxes are there? **(1)**

2. How would you define a tax? **(2)**

3. What aims can fiscal policy have other than raising revenue to meet government expenditure? **(3)**

4. How can taxation be used to lessen the inequality of incomes? **(3)**

5. What are the canons of taxation? **(4)**

6. To what extent can an expenditure tax be shifted? **(5)**

7. On what kind of goods should an expenditure tax be imposed if the Chancellor of the Exchequer wishes to raise revenue? **(5)**

8. What are the advantages and disadvantages of expenditure taxes? **(6)**

9. What are the economic effects of taxation? **(7)**

10. What is the National Debt? **(8)**

11. Distinguish between funded and unfunded debt. **(8)**

12. What are the advantages and disadvantages of rates as a form of taxation? **(9)**

CHAPTER XXII

MACRO-ECONOMICS

1. Investment and savings. *Investment* means adding to real capital, for example building a new factory. This gives rise to new incomes.

Of these new incomes, part will be *spent* on consumption goods and services; the remainder *not spent* on consumption goods and services will be *savings*.

The part of the incomes spent will add to the incomes of the suppliers of consumption goods and services.

The suppliers spend part of their new incomes and save the rest.

The suppliers of the suppliers now receive new incomes and they also spend and save.

This process will continue until *the total savings equal the amount of the original investment*.

The total incomes generated will be a multiple of the original investment. Thus, if an original investment of £100 generates incomes to the extent of £400, the multiplier is 4, that is, the total new incomes divided by the original investment.

The greater the *propensity to save* (the proportion of income that is saved), the lower the multiplier. The multiplier is the reciprocal of the propensity to save. In the example just given the propensity to save was $\frac{1}{4}$.

Although planned saving and planned investment will differ—they originate from different groups of people—yet realised savings will equal actual investment since investment affects incomes, which in turn affect savings.

2. Full employment. This has been defined as *a position where there are more jobs available than men unemployed*. It does not mean that everyone will be employed; there will be frictional unemployment.

Unemployment means a deficiency of incomes and hence a deficiency of demand.

Investment (for example, public works by the Government) will increase incomes and hence employment with a multiplier effect. Deficit budgeting is another method.

When resources are fully used and a position of full employment is reached, any attempt to increase incomes further will lead to inflation.

3. Inflation, deflation, and equilibrium.

Inflation occurs where there is a state of disequilibrium between purchasing power which is increasing and the output of goods and services which is not increasing to a corresponding extent; in other words when money incomes are increasing at a greater rate than productivity, thus leading to a general rise in prices.

The term "inflation" can also refer to (a) an increase in the amount of money (which does not necessarily mean a rise in prices) or (b) a rise in prices.

Deflation means either a decrease in the amount of money or a fall in prices.

Disinflation occurs when action is taken to counteract a state of inflation, lowering prices to an equilibrium level.

Deflation occurs if action is taken which lowers prices and output *below* the equilibrium level of full employment.

Reflation occurs if action is taken to raise prices and output to a level of full employment.

Inflation occurs if action is taken which raises prices *above* the level of those of full employment.

4. Rates of inflation.
Creeping inflation of about 2% per annum might be acceptable on the grounds that it acts as an incentive to investment. A rate greater than, say, 5% will undoubtedly cause hardship for those on fixed incomes, inflated wage demands from unions (anticipating further price rises), a worsening of the balance of payments and falling savings.

Hyper-inflation means that prices are rising faster and faster and the value of money is falling so fast that people are no longer prepared to accept money in payment for goods.

5. Causes of changes in price level.
(a) *Demand-pull.* An increase in demand not accompanied by an increase in supply which might come about because people were spending more and saving less or getting higher incomes or because increased credit facilities were available will cause prices to rise.

(*b*) *Cost-push*. Increased costs which could be caused by a rise in the prices of raw materials or by higher interest charges on loans or increased wage-rates (even when there is no increased demand for labour) are passed on to the consumer in the form of higher prices.

6. The Phillips curve. Contrary to Keynesian economics the economy does not change from price stability and unemployment to full employment and inflation (2). It changes slowly from one to the other.

The relation between price changes and the volume of unemployment can be shown by means of a Phillips curve (Fig. 19). The greater the unemployment the lower the rate of inflation.

٭ The Phillips curve is a description NOT an explanation.

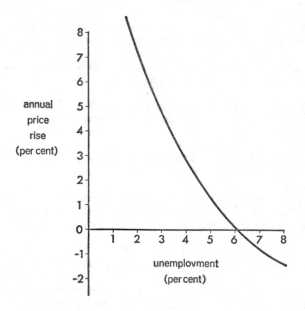

Fig. 19.—*The Phillips Curve.*

PROGRESS TEST 22

1. What is meant by investment? What is its relation to savings? (1)

2. What do you understand by the propensity to save? (1)

3. What is the multiplier? (1)

4. Explain the multiplier effect. (1)

5. How would you define full employment? (2)

6. Name two ways in which general unemployment may be solved. (2)

7. Distinguish between: (a) inflation; (b) reflation; (c) disinflation. (3)

8. When can inflation be (a) desirable; (b) highly undesirable; (c) ruinous? (4)

9. What do you understand by (a) demand-pull; (b) cost-push? (5)

10. What relationship is shown by a Phillips curve? (6)

CHAPTER XXIII

ECONOMIC FLUCTUATIONS

1. The trade cycle. Throughout the nineteenth century and during the twentieth, until the outbreak of World War I, economic activity fluctuated between boom and slump, the period between the booms being on an average eight years. This was the "trade cycle."

During the two World Wars and since the second, a higher level of production has been attained than ever before. Between the two wars there was a prolonged depression after a very short post-war boom.

The characteristics of the trade cycle:

(a) *A rapid decline from boom to slump* followed by a *period of depression.* This downward part of the cycle lasted on the average some four and a half years. This was followed by a *slow recovery* lasting about three and a half years.

(b) *The capital goods industries* are the *first to be depressed* and the *first to recover.*

(c) The *effects of depression* quickly *pass from country to country* (less income, fewer imports, less work for the exporting country).

2. The causes of economic fluctuations.

(a) *Durability of capital goods.* The labour force required to replace capital as it is consumed is only a fraction of that required to produce it originally.

EXAMPLE: 400 machines are produced in Year 1: 100 of these require replacement each year; 300 have a life of three years. The production required to replace the machines as they are worn out is as follows:

Year:	1	2	3	4	5	6	7
Production of machines:	400	100	100	400	100	100	400

Production and employment fluctuate with a three-year cycle.

(b) *Changes in expectation of demand* give rise to changes in investment. Changes in the demand for capital goods give rise to fluctuations because of the durability of capital equipment.

(c) *Planned savings exceed planned investment.* Excess savings mean a fall in demand and consequently a fall in the incomes of suppliers and a resultant fall in employment. The effect will be amplified by the multiplier effect.

(d) *Changes in the supply of money*, expansion leading to boom because of a lower rate of interest or restriction of credit leading to deflation and slump.

Many economists do not consider that changes in the supply of money *cause* fluctuations although they influence the extent of the movements.

3. Incomes and the trade cycle. The "boom" period of the cycle is one of high prices, profits, productivity, and employment; the "slump" period one of low prices, profits, productivity, and employment.

During the swing upwards, wages do not rise as fast as prices and therefore lag behind profits. The profits have not, however, increased to the extent they would appear to have done because prices are higher. Nevertheless receivers of profit are better off and wage earners less well off during a boom than during a slump. Receivers of fixed incomes are in the worst position of all.

During a slump the position is reversed. Prices are low and those in possession of fixed incomes are in the best position; wage earners, provided they retain their job, come next, and receivers of profits are in the worst position.

4. Unemployment. This may be of several types:

(a) *Frictional.* This is due to the immobility of labour between jobs. Even during full employment frictional unemployment will still exist, around 2% of the working population.

(b) *Seasonal.* Many industries are subject to seasonal fluctuations.

(c) *Structural.* This arises from permanent changes in demand, bringing about a change in the country's industrial structure.

(d) *Cyclical.* This occurs during the depression period of the trade cycle.

Local unemployment, usually structural, is not dealt with as if it were general unemployment. Measures used for correcting general unemployment, if used to correct local unemployment, would lead to inflation.

The *Local Employment Acts* 1960–1972 permit the Government to bring work to areas where a high rate of unemployment exists.

A grant to a firm to expand in such an area and the refusal of an I.D.C. (industrial development certificate) to expand on its existing site is one method of doing this

5. The recession-expansion cycle. Expansion of credit to increase output may lead to inflation and the consequent higher prices may in turn lead to balance of payment difficulties. To correct a deficit on the balance of payments, credit is restricted and prices and output fall. The fall in output will probably be greater than is desired and credit is once more expanded.

PROGRESS TEST 23

1. What is the trade cycle? (1)
2. What are the causes of economic fluctuations? (2)
3. What effect have changes in the level of economic activity upon the relative incomes of wage earners and receivers of profit? (3)
4. What is meant by structural unemployment? How can it be dealt with? (4)
5. What is meant by: (*a*) frictional (*b*) cyclical unemployment? (4)

EXAMINATION TECHNIQUE

SOME students consider that examinations in economics can be passed by "flannelling"; others think it is only a matter of common sense (which is, in fact, a scarce commodity); and some think that all that is necessary is to read the "serious" newspapers.

This is not so. The *first requisite* for examination success is to *know your subject*.

A large number of students find it easy to understand economics and hence think nothing need be learned. It is too late when you find your memory has failed you in the examination room. You must, therefore, *learn and continually revise* (this book is compiled in such a way as to enable you to do just that).

Often a student fails to check his knowledge as he continues his studies. He then comes up against unnecessary difficulties because he has erroneous ideas about the subject or has failed to learn some vital step. And, of course, if he does not check his knowledge he will not know if he has forgotten some very necessary information for examination success; he will not know if his answers in the examination are right or not.

Test yourself by means of the Progress Tests. It is not sufficient to just look at a question and say, "Oh yes! I know that one." This might merely mean that the question is understood, or that the student remembers having dealt with the subject-matter of the question. *Write out the answer without reference to textbook or notes and then check.*

But, having fully prepared yourself for the examination (examiners report that *many* students fail to prepare adequately), it is still possible to fail. There is, in fact, an examination technique.

The following slogan might be useful to remember when dealing with any question: *answer the question, the whole question, and nothing but the question.*

"Answer the question" might seem superfluous advice, but too often a question is misread and an entirely different question actually answered. However good *this* answer, it cannot earn marks. It is tantamount to saying to the examiner, "I don't know the answer to your question so I have written an answer to a question I do know." *Read the question carefully and make sure you understand it before attempting an answer.*

"The whole question." A question often consists of more than one part. Check that you have answered all the examiner has asked for.

"Nothing but the question": irrelevancies earn no marks and cost time; a most uneconomic policy. There is a tendency to expand an answer on that part about which most is known. This leads to overstepping the limits of the subject to be dealt with. So do *keep to the point.*

Examination procedure.

(1) *Read the instructions carefully and follow them absolutely.* Note particularly the number of questions to be done, and if any are compulsory.

(2) *Allocate your time.* If, for example, the time allowed is two hours and five questions carrying equal marks have to be done, there would be 24 minutes for each question. But of this 24 minutes, perhaps 3 minutes might be required for planning your answer and another 3 minutes for reading it through when completed.

Do not spend more than your allotted time on any question. If it is not completed in that time leave a space and go on to another question. Come back to it if you can gain time on the other questions. More marks are obtained on two half-answered questions than on one completely answered question. The number of marks earned for each minute spent on any question is subject to the law of diminishing returns.

(3) *Decide which question you will answer first.* This will be the one you can answer most confidently. Don't worry about the others. Answering the first question well—and there must be at least one you can answer well if you have paid some attention to your course—will settle "examination nerves."

(4) *Plan the answer to this question.* Jot down all the points that occur to you. Some will possibly be irrelevant; cross them out. Put the others in a logical order. Usually there will only be about three or four points. Devote a paragraph to each one. Choose a good introductory sentence or two and end with a good summary or conclusion. Time spent on planning is well

spent. It ensures that your answer covers the question and does not contain irrelevant topics. It also enables you to give a logically developed answer; this earns marks.

(5) *Write the answer to the question.* Make sure you do not overstep the allocated time. Many students work best when working "against the clock."

(6) *Read your answer.* When reading it imagine yourself to be the examiner. Be critical and correct errors. This step, often neglected, is *very* important. It is so easy to write one thing and intend to write something entirely different. Leaving out a word, *e.g.* "not," may have the effect of turning a "pass" into a failure.

(7) *Pass on to the next question.* Read carefully, plan, write, and read over your answer.

(8) *Continue in this way until all requisite questions are answered.*

(9) *Complete any answers left unfinished.* If there is not sufficient time to complete any answer, finish it in note form or indicate how the answer would be completed. This will often earn useful marks.

Use of diagrams. Use diagrams wherever they can make a useful contribution to your answer. They must be neat and add to the clarity of the answer. But if a diagram gains marks quickly, remember that an incorrect diagram—and particularly a meaningless one—will lose marks equally quickly. Do not add a diagram if it adds nothing to your answer.

TEST PAPERS

Do not attempt these papers until you have thoroughly mastered the course and are able to answer satisfactorily all the Progress Tests.

Do each paper under *strict examination conditions*, bearing in mind the hints on examination techniques in Appendix I.

Allow TWO hours for each paper. Answer FIVE questions.

Test 1

1. "The supply curve is a cost curve." Explain.

2. Why do some countries have a high national income while others have a very low one?

3. "The marginal productivity theory of wages is a static theory" (Lord Keynes). Comment.

4. In what circumstances do you think the Government might intervene when a firm is choosing a site for a new factory?

5. Compare and contrast the functions of a central bank with those of a commercial bank.

6. What are the sources of savings in Great Britain?

7. What is meant by the terms of trade? Is an improvement in the terms of trade always desirable?

Test 2

1. Price is determined by supply and demand. But what determines supply and demand?

2. What happens to the cost per unit of output as a firm gets bigger? Give reasons for your answer.

3. Any factor of production can earn rent. Explain how this can be so.

4. How are wages determined in an occupation that has no trade union?

5. A banker will say that he cannot create money. He can only lend money if he has money to lend. Economists on the other hand say that banks create money. Who is right?

6. What is meant by a deficit balance on the balance of payments? If such a balance persisted over a fairly long period what action would have to be taken?

7. If you were devising a system of taxation what principles would you adopt?

Test 3

1. What are (a) internal economies (b) external economies? In what way do they lower costs?

2. Give a short account of the way the population of England and Wales has grown over the last 200 years.

3. What are the effects of a change in the price of any commodity?

4. When are monopolies beneficial to the consumer?

5. What special institutions have been formed to provide medium- and long-term capital because the existing machinery was not considered adequate?

6. What is meant by the value of money? How can changes in its value be measured?

7. What are the advantages and disadvantages of a purchase tax from the point of view of the Chancellor of the Exchequer?

Test 4

1. Lord Robbins has described economics as a science. Why is it a science and what kind of science is it?

2. What is (a) a preference share (b) a debenture (c) an ordinary share?

3. What is the relationship between the elasticity of demand for a commodity and the revenue obtained from its sale?

4. Do earnings increase if wages increase?

5. Why is the long-term rate of interest different from the short-term rate? Which is the higher?

6. What is a Treasury bill and what part does it play in the work of the discount houses?

7. What are the causes of unemployment? What measures can be taken to remedy it?

Test 5

1. What are the principal types of unemployment considered with reference to their major causes?

(*Institute of Bankers*)

2. What part do capital movements play in the United Kingdom Balance of Payments?　　　(*G.C.E.* "*A*" *Level*)

3. What do you understand by the market for new capital?
　　　　　　　　　　　　　　　　　　　(*G.C.E.* "*A*" *Level*)

4. Import controls are a way of correcting an unsatisfactory balance of payments. Discuss the objections to their use.
　　　　　　　　　　　　　　　　　　(*Institute of Bankers*)

5. Is rent a cost of production?　　　(*I.C.S.A. Inter*)

6. "Banks do not create money; they only lend money which has been deposited with them." Discuss.　(*I.C.S.A. Inter*)

7. Examine the economic effects of the present trend towards an ageing population in the United Kingdom.
　　　　　　　　　　　　　　　　　　(*G.C.E.* "*A*" *Level*)

Test 6

1. "Unemployment persists only because labour is immobile and trade unions refuse to accept cuts in money wages." Discuss.　　　　　　　　　　　　(*G.C.E.* "*A*" *Level*)

2. "While the accuracy of the quantity equation in the theory of money is beyond dispute its usefulness is not so certain." Discuss.　　　　　　　　　(*G.C.E.* "*A*" *Level*)

3. Describe the practical use of index numbers. How are they constructed?　　　　　　　　(*Institute of Bankers*)

4. What are the advantages of the limited liability company over other types of business organisation?　(*I.C.S.A. Inter*)

5. Illustrate in diagrammatic form the equilibrium between demand and supply under conditions of perfect competition and decreasing cost. Explain the various parts and the meaning of the diagram.　　　　　　　　(*I.C.S.A. Inter*)

6. What main economic factors affect the standard of living?
　　　　　　　　　　　　　　　　　　(*Institute of Bankers*)

7. Why do wages vary between different occupations?
　　　　　　　　　　　　　　　　　　(*I.C.S.A. Inter*)

INDEX